BRIAN FEROLDI

WHY DOES THE STOCK MARKET GO UP?

Everything You Should Have Been Taught
About Investing In School, But Weren't

ISBN:
978-1-7350661-6-5 (Paperback)
978-1-7350661-7-2 (Hardcover)
978-1-7350661-5-8 (eBook)

Library of Congress Control Number: 2021947458

All content reflects our opinion at a given time and can change as time progresses. All information should be taken as an opinion and should not be misconstrued for professional or legal advice. The contents of this book are informational in nature and are not legal or tax advice, and the authors and publishers are not engaged in the provision of legal, tax, or any other advice.

Front cover image and book design by Giada Creative LLC

Printed by Choose FI Media, Inc., in the United States of America.
First printing edition 2021.

Choose FI Media, Inc.
P.O. Box 3982
Glen Allen, VA 23058
www.choosefi.com
Twitter Direct Messages: @choosefi

ATTENTION: Quantity discounts are available to your company, educational institution, or writing organization for reselling, educational purposes, subscription incentives, gifts, or fundraiser campaigns.

Email: brian@brianferoldi.com
Twitter: @brianferoldi
YouTube: /brianferoldiyt
LinkedIn: /in/brianferoldi/
Instagram: @brianferoldi
Web: brianferoldi.com

DEDICATION

This book is dedicated to everyone that uses their free time
to enhance their financial knowledge.

In other words, this book is dedicated to you.

GIVEAWAY

Thank you so much for buying this book. It means a lot to me.

As a special thank you for your purchase, please visit **brianferoldi.com/thankyou** to receive:

1. A full list of recommended free tools that can help you invest

2. A bonus chapter where I discuss my biggest investing mistakes of all time

3. A bonus interview where I talk with Brad Barrett and Jonathan Mendonsa of the ChooseFI podcast about the key concepts discussed in this book

TABLE OF CONTENTS

INTRODUCTION

I worked as a golf caddy in high school.

During a round, one of the golfers stopped at the clubhouse. When he returned, he told his fellow golfers "You're not going to believe this, but the Dow Jones is up 300 points today!"

The other golfers replied with "You're kidding!", "Wow!", and "That's amazing!" They all seemed to be pleasantly surprised with this news.

Me? I was confused.

I had heard the term "Dow Jones" before, but I had no clue what it meant. I knew it had *something* to do with the stock market. I also knew that it was good news when it went up.

Beyond that, I was clueless.

I know that my experience is not unique. Many people hear about the stock market's daily moves in the news. And yet, most of us have **no clue** what any of it means.

Most people can't even answer basic questions like:

- What is a stock?
- What is the Dow Jones Industrial Average?
- Why does the stock market go up and down?

That's a tragedy, because the stock market is **the greatest wealth creation machine of all time**. It has helped millions of ordinary people to build wealth and reach their financial goals.

What's more, most Americans have money in the stock market,

even if they don't realize it. Tens of millions of Americans need the stock market to rise in order to fund their retirement, buy a house, pay for college, or achieve some other financial dream.

I am one of those weird people that is naturally interested in the stock market. That has led me to consume every bit of financial content that I could get my hands on over the last 20 years.

I've read hundreds of books about investing. I've listened to thousands of podcast episodes about money. I've spent countless hours on message boards that discuss the nitty gritty details of the stock market.

That thirst for knowledge allowed me to answer all of the questions that I had about the stock market when I was a beginner.

And yet, during those decades of learning, I've never come across a book that did a great job of answering **the most important question** that I had about the stock market:

Why does the stock market go up?

You can't invest with confidence if you don't know the answer to that question.

If you don't understand **why** the stock market goes up, then you won't know **why** it crashes sometimes or **why** it has always bounced back.

That missing answer is the reason why the book you are holding exists.

The mission of this book is to demystify the stock market. My aim is to explain how the stock market works in simple terms so that everyone can invest with confidence.

In other words, this is the book that **I wish I had** when I first started investing 20 years ago.

HOW TO USE
THIS BOOK

This book was designed to make it as easy as possible for anyone to understand the most important concepts about the stock market. Each short chapter answers one important question about the stock market and investing.

Parts 1 through 10 are designed to take you through a journey of discovery and understanding. We'll regularly reference a made-up business called Best Coffee Company as an example. It is best to read these parts sequentially.

The last section of the book is titled "Common Questions - Answered." This is a compilation of the most common questions that I have heard from new investors over the years. Please read these in any order that you wish, or simply use the section as a reference guide.

Once you are done with the book, keep it on your nightstand, bookshelf, or coffee table so that you can go back and review any of these chapters as you start to invest.

CHAPTER 1

WHY SHOULD I CARE ABOUT THE STOCK MARKET?

Most people do not care about the stock market. It's not hard to figure out why.

The stock market appears to move up and down randomly. It doesn't seem to be linked to what's happening in the real world at all.

The media only tends to make a big deal out of the stock market when it crashes, like it did most recently in 2000, 2008, and 2020.

The movie industry hasn't helped, either. Popular movies like *The Big Short*, *Margin Call*, *Boiler Room*, and *The Wolf of Wall Street* all make the stock market seem like a big gambling machine.

I've heard people say things like:

- "The stock market is rigged."
- "Wall Street rips off Main Street."
- "The stock market is just a playground for the wealthy."

That's a shame, because the truth is that the stock market is the greatest wealth creation machine of all time.

Let me repeat that: **The stock market is the greatest wealth creation machine of all time**.

The stock market has enabled *millions* of ordinary people to build wealth and achieve their financial goals.

To show how, we'll look at one example of how the stock market can help an average person realize their financial goals.

Let's say a fictitious person named Aaron started his career in 1981, which is the same year that 401(k)s were created. His starting salary was $26,000, which was just under the average family income in the U.S. at the time.

Aaron was OK with money, but he wasn't great. He lived paycheck-to-paycheck, but he always paid off his debt on time.

Thankfully, Aaron made one great financial decision. When he started his career, he put $400 per month into his company's 401(k). He invested it all in funds that grew at the same rate as the overall United States stock market.

Then he completely forgot about his 401(k). He didn't even bother to check his statements.

After 39 years of working, he finally took a look at his 401(k) balance.

How much money was in Aaron's 401(k)?

$3,013,537

Aaron was shocked! And also confused. How had he become a multi-millionaire?

He did some quick math. His $400 per month only amounted to $191,600. Where did the extra $2.82 million come from?

The answer is the greatest wealth creation machine of all time: **the stock market**.

The U.S. stock market grew at a rate of about 11% per year during Aaron's career. When that growth rate was combined with his savings of $400 per month, his investment **portfolio** got bigger at a faster and faster rate each year—although the growth didn't occur in a straight line.

After the first year, Aaron had invested a total of $4,800. However, the stock market didn't move much during the year, so his portfolio was only worth $4,823.

By the second year, Aaron had invested a total of $9,600. The stock market was up during this time, so his portfolio value was lifted to $11,383.

After five years, Aaron had invested a total of $24,000. The stock market went up a lot over those five years, which grew his portfolio to $37,594.

After a decade, Aaron had invested a total of $48,000. The stock market went up some more, so his portfolio grew to $101,208.

That's when things started to get interesting. Since Aaron's portfolio was now worth $101,208 and it was still growing about 11% annually, *the gains from his investments were adding more value to his portfolio than his $400 per month contribution.*

The stock market continued to go up during the 1990s. By the end of his second decade of investing, Aaron's portfolio was worth $696,839.

A portfolio is a collection of financial assets that are owned by an investor.

The 2000s were a tough period for the stock market. There were two big declines in 2000 and 2008. At the end of Aaron's third decade of investing, his portfolio only grew a little bit and was worth $793,479.

However, the stock market's growth rate picked up in the 2010s. By the end of 2020, Aaron had invested a total of $191,600, but the portfolio was worth $3,013,537.

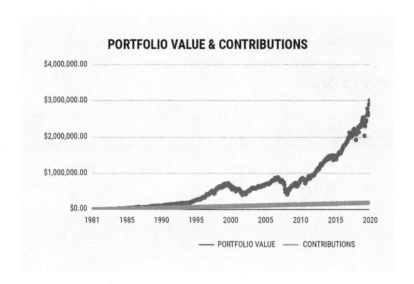

You might be thinking Aaron's results were a fluke. Maybe he just got lucky and invested during a good period for the stock market.

History says otherwise.

The U.S. stock market has gone up about 10% per year dating back to 1871.

If you invested just $1 in the U.S. stock market in 1871, **you'd now have more than $580,000**.

And keep in mind that this period included a depression, two world wars, Presidential assassinations, pandemics, terrorist attacks, and numerous recessions.

This is why the stock market is the greatest wealth creation machine of all time. The stock market can allow anyone to turn small amounts of money into life-changing wealth over time.

And—like it or not—**money affects us all**.

Money determines where you live, the food that you eat, the education that your children receive, the healthcare you can access, the life experiences you can have, and much, much more.

Even if you have no interest in material possessions, building wealth is one of the best things that you can do to improve your family's circumstances.

And there's no better tool for building wealth than the stock market.

If you're still not convinced, consider this: **you might already have money in the stock market, even if you don't know it**. Gallup estimates that more than half of Americans currently own stocks, mostly through retirement plans.

If you have a:

- 401(k)
- 403(b)
- 457 Plan
- Brokerage Account
- Employee Stock Purchase Plan (ESPP)
- Financial Advisor
- Index Fund
- Individual Retirement Arrangement (IRA)
- Mutual Fund
- Pension
- ROTH IRA
- ROTH 401(k)
- SARSEP Plan
- SEP Plan

- Simple IRA
- Thrift Savings Plan

...the odds are good that you are already invested in the stock market.

You have this amazing, wealth-creating tool at your disposal, but you may not know how it works or how to use it.

Once you understand the basics, you will learn how to harness the stock market's awesome wealth-building power.

And don't be intimated; the basics are not complicated. If you can understand 5th grade math, you can understand how the stock market works. You can also learn how to turn small amounts of money into life-changing amounts of wealth.

That is why you should care about it.

PART 1
STOCK MARKET BASICS

CHAPTER 2

WHAT IS A STOCK?

Let's say three friends named Natalie, Ethan, and Lauren decide to open up a coffee shop together. They name their new business Best Coffee Company and estimate that it will cost $10,000 to get the coffee shop up and running.

Natalie has $6,000 to invest. Ethan has $3,000. Lauren only has $1,000.

- How much of Best Coffee Company will Natalie, Ethan, and Lauren own?

- How will Natalie, Ethan, and Lauren protect themselves from being sued if one of their customers spills hot coffee on themself?

A corporation is a legal entity that is separate from its owners. Corporations are owned by shareholders. The shareholders have a legal claim on the corporation's assets and profits but are not personally liable for the company's debts or actions.

Business owners have been dealing with questions like these for centuries. This is why **corporations** were invented.

Corporations make it easy for businesses to raise money from investors. They also offer legal protection to the investors in case the business gets sued or goes bankrupt.

One way that corporations raise money is by selling **stock**, which is also called 'equity' or 'shares'. A stock represents *partial ownership* of a corporation. The owners of the stock are called 'stockholders' or 'shareholders'.

The shareholders have a claim on a *portion* of the company's assets (what it owns) and its profits. Shareholders also get to vote on how the business is managed.

A stock (which is also known as equity) is a financial security that represents the ownership of a fraction of a corporation.

Natalie, Ethan, and Lauren decide to turn Best Coffee Shop into a corporation. They decide to sell stock in the new business for $1 per share.

	Natalie	Ethan	Lauren	Total
Initial Investment	$6,000	$3,000	$1,000	$10,000
Shares Owned	6,000	3,000	1,000	10,000

Stocks make it easy for investors to figure out how much of the company they own. To find this out, the owners simply divide the number of shares that they own by the total number of shares.

For example, Natalie, who contributed 60% of the start-up funding, owns 60% equity in the company. If there are 10,000 shares, then she owns 6,000 of them:

	Natalie	Ethan	Lauren
Shares Owned	6,000	3,000	1,000
Total Shares of Best Coffee Company	10,000	10,000	10,000
Ownership Percentage	60%	30%	10%

Here's what the ownership looks like on a pie chart:

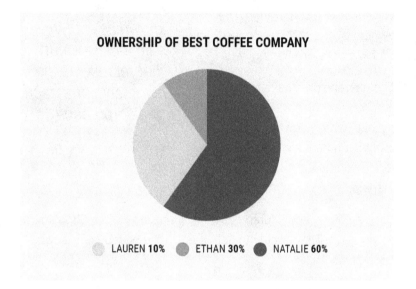

OWNERSHIP OF BEST COFFEE COMPANY

LAUREN **10%**   ETHAN **30%**   NATALIE **60%**

This is one reason stocks were invented. Stocks help investors understand how much of a corporation they own.

CHAPTER 3

WHY DO STOCKS HAVE VALUE?

Let's continue with the example from the last chapter. Let's say that Best Coffee Company is successful. It makes $5,000 in profit during its first year.

Natalie, Ethan, and Lauren decide to take the $5,000 in profit and pay it to themselves. In corporation speak, this is called paying a **dividend**.

A dividend is when a company gives some of its profits—which are also called 'earnings' or 'net income'—back to its shareholders.

A dividend is a portion of a company's profits that are paid out to its shareholders.

How much of that $5,000 should go to Natalie, Ethan, and Lauren? To find out, we divide the total dividend payment by the total number of shares.

$$\frac{\$5,000 \leftarrow \text{Total dividend payment}}{10,000 \leftarrow \text{Total number of shares}} = \$0.50 \text{ per share}$$

Next, we multiply the dividend payment per share by the number of shares that each of the shareholders own.

Natalie would receive a $3,000 payment. Ethan would receive a $1,500 payment. Lauren would receive a $500 payment.

	Natalie	Ethan	Lauren	Total
Shares Owned	6,000	3,000	1,000	10,000
Dividend Per Share	$0.50	$0.50	$0.50	$0.50
Total Payment	$3,000	$1,500	$500	$5,000

Would you like to own shares of Best Coffee Company?

You should! It's a successful business that paid each of its investors $0.50 for every share of stock that they own in just one year. That can be very valuable to you as a shareholder.

What if Best Coffee Company makes another $5,000 in profit next year? What if it makes $10,000 in profit the year after that?

Would you even be willing to pay Natalie, Ethan, or Lauren to buy some of their stock? If yes, then the stock has value.

That is why stocks have value. When you own a stock, you have a legal claim on a portion of a company's assets and profits. If that business makes money, then that money belongs to the shareholders.

Importantly, profits are not always paid out to shareholders in the form of dividends. Often a company's management team will keep its profits inside the business and use them to buy equipment, pay off debt, hire employees, or for other uses.

However, no matter what the company does with its profits, the profits belong to the shareholders.

That is why stocks have value.

CHAPTER 4

WHAT IS THE STOCK MARKET?

Let's keep the Best Coffee Company example going. Lauren needs money and decides that she wants to sell her shares in Best Coffee Company. However, Natalie and Ethan do not want to buy them from her.

Lauren has to find another investor that is interested in buying her shares. How will she do that? This is a problem that shareholders have been dealing with for centuries.

In 1792, a group of investors from New York City got together and solved this problem. This group gathered on a road called Wall Street to buy and sell—or "exchange"—shares in businesses with each other.

That's all a "**stock market**" is; it's a place where businesses and investors can connect with each other in order to buy and sell stocks.

It's kind of like a farmer's market, but instead of trading money for food, you trade money for shares in businesses.

The group of investors who were exchanging stocks in New York

A stock market is place where businesses and investors connect with each other to buy, sell, and issue shares of publically held companies.

grew over time. It still exists today. It is known as the New York Stock Exchange (NYSE), which is the largest stock market in the world.

Lots of other stock markets have since popped up all around the world. Some of the big ones include the Hong Kong Stock Exchange, Shanghai Stock Exchange, Tokyo Stock Exchange, London Stock Exchange, and the NASDAQ stock market (more on this in Chapter 7).

CHAPTER 5

WHAT IS THE DOW JONES INDUSTRIAL AVERAGE?

In 1896, Charles Dow was an editor at *The Wall Street Journal*.

Dow had a problem. His paper reported stock prices each day, but there wasn't an easy way for him to recap the market's daily ups and downs for his readers.

Dow asked his business associate Edward Jones for help. The two of them invented a solution.

Dow and Jones added up the share price of 12 of the biggest and most popular publicly traded companies at the time. The total was then divided by 12. The result was reported as a proxy for what happened in the stock market that day.

Dow and Jones named their invention the "Dow Jones Industrial Average." It is also referred to as the "Dow Jones" or just "Dow." It has been reported to the public every business day since it was created.

The Dow Jones Industrial Average is what's known as a **stock market index**. An index is a group of stocks that are combined to figure out whether the stock market as a whole is going up or down. It is a way to track the performance of the stock market.

A stock market index is a basket of stocks that are used to help investors track the performance of the stock market as a whole.

The business world has changed a lot since 1896, so the Dow Jones has adapted to keep up. In 1928, the Dow was expanded to include 30 companies instead of just 12. Every few years some of the declining businesses in the Dow Jones are removed and are replaced by businesses that are growing. This helps to ensure that the biggest and most successful companies of the day are always included in the Dow Jones. As of 2021, the Dow includes businesses like **Apple** (NASDAQ:AAPL), **Disney** (NYSE:DIS), and **Home Depot** (NYSE:HD).

On May 26, 1896, the average price of the original 12 Dow Jones Industrial Average stocks was $40.94. The Dow has grown at a rate of about 10% per year ever since.

A price-weighted index is a type of stock market index in which each stock is weighted by the current share price. This means that stocks with a higher share price have more influence over the index than stocks with a lower share price.

That might not sound like much, but those gains have added up to create *huge* growth.

The Dow Jones has become one of the most well-known stock market indexes in the world. However, the Dow Jones also has critics that point out two big flaws.

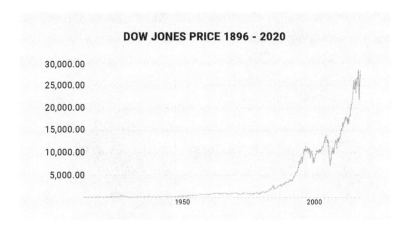

First, the Dow Jones only tracks 30 companies. That's only a tiny fraction of the 6,000 publicly traded companies that exist in the U.S. alone. Critics argue the Dow Jones does not accurately represent the entire stock market.

Second, the Dow Jones is calculated by using the dollar price of each stock. The Dow Jones ignores the *size* of each business. This means that a stock that is trading for $100 per share will have *10 times more influence* over the Dow Jones than a stock trading at $10 per share.

That's why the Dow is called a **price-weighted index**. The dollar price of each stock is what matters, not the size of each business.

To see why some investors think that this is a problem, let's review the stock price from two Dow Jones stocks—**McDonald's** (NYSE:MCD) and **Intel** (NASDAQ:INTC)—in October 2020:

October, 2020	McDonald's (NYSE:MCD)	Intel (NASDAQ:INTC)
Share Price	$228	$54
Business Size	$170 billion	$222 billion

McDonald's was $52 billion *smaller* than Intel, but its share price was about four times *higher*. This means that the price movement of McDonald's stock had a four times greater influence over the performance of the Dow Jones than Intel's stock, even though Intel was a larger company!

For these reasons, many professional investors do not believe that the Dow Jones is a good index for tracking the overall movements of the U.S. stock market.

WHAT IS THE S&P 500?

In 1923, the Standard Statistics Company created a new stock market index. Their goal was to compete with the Dow Jones Industrial Average, which was popular with investors. To stand out, Standard Statistics decided to use data on 233 companies instead of just 30 like the Dow Jones.

Years later, the Standard Statistics Company merged with Poor's Publishing to create the Standard & Poor's (S&P) company. In 1957, S&P made a few changes to its stock market index that would allow it to better compete with the Dow Jones.

First, S&P increased the number of companies that it tracked from 233 to 500.

Second, S&P let larger companies have more influence over the index's movements than smaller companies. S&P judged the size of each business by using its **market capitalization**, which is the total dollar market value of a company's equity. This is called a **capitalization-weighted index**.

On March 4, 1957, the S&P 500 was officially launched.

Each year, some weak businesses are removed from the S&P 500 and are replaced by stronger businesses. This helps to ensure

Market capitalization is the current dollar value of a company's equity. It is found by multiplying the total number of a company's shares by the current market price of one share.

that the biggest and most successful companies of the day are always included in the S&P 500. This steady annual turnover has caused the S&P 500 to look a lot different today than it did 60 years ago.

In 2021, large companies like **Apple** (NASDAQ:AAPL), **Microsoft** (NASDAQ:MSFT), and **Amazon** (NASDAQ:AMZN) had market values that exceeded $1 trillion. That causes them to have much more influence over the index than smaller companies like **Hanesbrands** (NYSE:HBI) and **Under Armour** (NYSE:UA) which are worth less than $10 billion. This is why many investors like that the S&P 500 is a capitalization-weighted index.

A capitalization-weighted index is a stock market index in which each stock is weighted by its current market capitalization. This means that larger companies have more influence over the index than smaller companies.

This chart shows the relative size of all of the companies in the S&P 500 as of December 31st, 2020. Notice how Amazon, Google, and Tesla are much bigger than smaller companies.

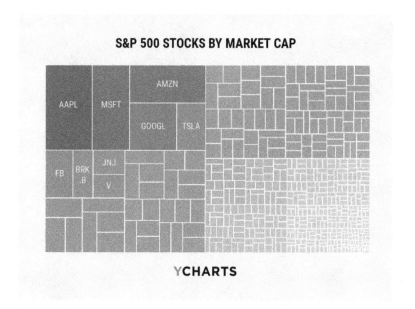

S&P 500 STOCKS BY MARKET CAP

YCHARTS

The S&P 500 has grown at a rate of about 10% per year since it was created. That has led it to significantly increase in value over the past 60 years.

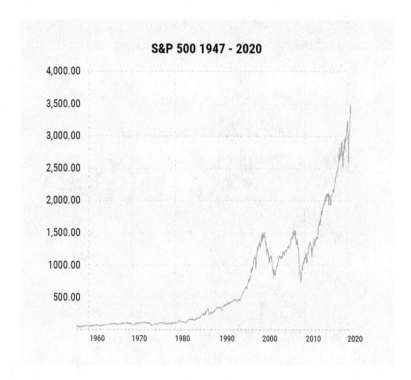

The S&P 500 gradually became more popular with investors. Today, many investors believe that it is a much better index for tracking the overall movements of the U.S. stock market than the Dow Jones Industrial Average.

THE RULE OF 72

A quick way to figure out how many years it will take you to double your money is to use The Rule of 72. Simply divide 72 by the annual interest rate. The result is the number of years that it will take you to double your money.

For example, if you earn a 10% annualized return, then it will take about 7.2 years to double your money (72 divided by 10 = 7.2). If you earn an 8% annualized return, it will take 9 years (72 divided by 8 = 9).

The Rule of 72 isn't perfectly accurate, but it is an easy way to get a fast estimate.

CHAPTER 7

WHAT IS THE NASDAQ?

Computers became a lot more advanced during the 1950s and 1960s. By the early 1970s, people who worked on Wall Street started to experiment with computers to see if they could be used to improve stock trading.

At the time, there wasn't a good way to get stock price information— or stock "quotes"—to all investors at the same time. This made buying and selling stocks inefficient and expensive.

The National Association of Securities Dealers (NASD), an agency that oversees the buying and selling of stocks, decided that computers could be used to solve this problem.

The NASD created a brand-new stock exchange in 1971. This new stock exchange would allow investors to buy and sell stocks on computers that were connected to each other. They called this new stock market the **N**ational **A**ssociation of **S**ecurities **D**ealers **A**utomated **Q**uotations, or **NASDAQ**.

The NASDAQ stock exchange offered many advantages over other stock exchanges. Since all of the buying and selling was done on computers there was no need to have a physical trading floor. Accurate prices could also be viewed by all investors at the same time.

These benefits convinced many companies to list their stocks on the NASDAQ stock exchange instead of the New York Stock Exchange. This includes many well-known tech companies such as **Intel** (NASDAQ:INTC), **Microsoft** (NASDAQ:MSFT), and **Adobe** (NASDAQ:ADBE).

The inventors of the NASDAQ stock exchange also created an index that tracked the price movements of all the companies that were listed on the exchange. They called this new index the **NASDAQ Composite Index**. Today, there are more than 3,200 businesses that make up the NASDAQ Composite Index.

Like the S&P 500, the NASDAQ Composite Index is a capitalization-weighted index. This means that larger companies have a bigger influence over the movement of the NASDAQ Composite Index than smaller companies.

Over time, many other stock exchanges began to offer electronic trading.

Here's where things can get a little confusing; the term "NASDAQ" is often used as shorthand to refer to both the NASDAQ stock exchange *and* the NASDAQ Composite Index.

However, whenever you hear the term "NASDAQ" mentioned in the news, it usually refers to the Nasdaq Composite Index.

The NASDAQ composite index is a stock market index that tracks the price movements of all the companies that are listed on the NASDAQ stock exchange.

PART 1 REVIEW

- Stock represents partial ownership of a corporation.

- Stocks have value because the owner has a legal claim on a portion of the company's profits and assets.

- The stock market is a place where businesses and investors can connect with each other in order to buy and sell stocks.

- A stock exchange is a place where stocks are listed so they can be bought or sold by public investors. The two largest stock exchanges in the world are the New York Stock Exchange (NYSE) and NASDAQ Stock Exchange.

- A stock market index is a basket of stocks that are used to track the performance of the stock market as a whole. The three most popular stock market indexes in the U.S. are the Dow Jones Industrial Average, the S&P 500, and the NASDAQ Composite.

	Dow Jones Industrial Average	S&P 500	Nasdaq Composite
Date Created	1896	1957	1971
Weighting System	Price-Weighted	Capitalization-weighted	Capitalization-weighted
Holdings	30	500	~3,200

PART 2

GOING PUBLIC

WHY DO COMPANIES GO PUBLIC?

Let's return to our Best Coffee Company example.

Natalie, Ethan, and Lauren believe that they can grow Best Coffee Company's profits by opening up new locations. They decide to build 10 new stores. The cost to build each store is $10,000, so they need $100,000.

How are they going to get the $100,000?

The first option is to borrow the money. Best Coffee Company could get a loan from a bank for $100,000. However, this option isn't ideal because debt has to be paid back to the bank on a preset schedule with interest.

What if the new stores are not as profitable as the first store? What if the new stores take a long time to reach profitability? These questions make taking on debt risky.

The second option is to add new investors. Best Coffee Company could create new shares of stock and sell them to new investors to raise the $100,000.

The upside of selling new stock is that the money *doesn't have to be paid back*. The downside is there will be more investors to split the company's profits with.

Let's say Natalie, Ethan, and Lauren decide to raise the $100,000 by taking Best Coffee Company public. They hire investment bankers who suggest that the new public investors will be willing to buy 10,000 shares of stock for $10 each. That will get them the $100,000 they want.

Natalie, Ethan, and Lauren agree to the terms and take Best Coffee Company public.

Before going public Natalie owns 60%, Ethan owns 30%, and Lauren owns 10%.

	Natalie	Ethan	Lauren	Total
Shares Owned	6,000	3,000	1,000	10,000
Ownership Percentage	60%	30%	10%	100%

Best Coffee Company then creates 10,000 new shares of stock and sells them to public investors. Afterwards, Natalie still owns 6,000 shares, but her ownership position has been reduced to just 30%. Ethan still owns 3,000 shares, but his ownership position has been reduced to 15%. Lauren still owns 1,000 shares, but her ownership position has been reduced to just 5%.

	Natalie	Ethan	Lauren	Public Investors	Total
Shares Owned	6,000	3,000	1,000	10,000	20,000
Ownership Percentage	30%	15%	5%	50%	100%

Best Coffee Company gets the $100,000 that it wants to build the new stores. This is the primary reason why companies go public: to raise money. That money could be used to hire workers, buy equipment, pay off debt, or for many other things.

The downside to going public is that the original owners no longer own 100% of the business. Natalie, Ethan, and Lauren only own *half* of Best Coffee Company after it went public in this example. This is because of an effect called **dilution**.

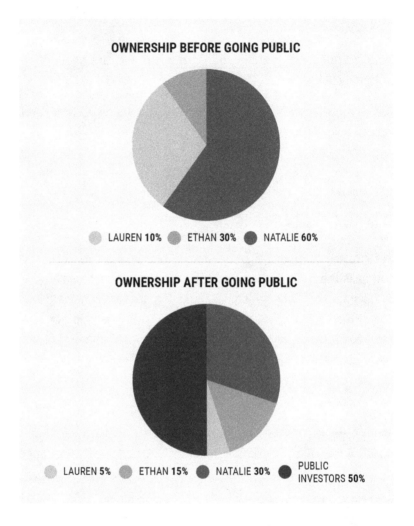

OWNERSHIP BEFORE GOING PUBLIC

LAUREN **10%**   ETHAN **30%**   NATALIE **60%**

OWNERSHIP AFTER GOING PUBLIC

LAUREN **5%**   ETHAN **15%**   NATALIE **30%**   PUBLIC INVESTORS **50%**

This is what happened when **Starbucks** (NASDAQ:SBUX) went public in 1992. At the time, Starbucks had 140 locations, but its management team wanted to double the number of stores in two years. To raise the money needed to build those new stores, Starbucks created and sold new shares of stock to the public. This is called an **Initial Public Offering (IPO)**.

CHAPTER 8: WHY DO COMPANIES GO PUBLIC?

Starbucks created 1,470,000 new shares of stock and sold them for $17 each. This raised $25 million. At the time of the IPO, Starbucks' existing shareholders were diluted by about 12%.

Dilution occurs when a company creates new shares of stock, which has the effect of lowering the ownership percentage of the company's existing stockholders.

Starbucks' shareholders were OK with this dilution because they believed that the money they would receive from the IPO would enable the company to build new stores and expand rapidly. That would cause the value of Starbucks to rise over time and would create high returns for investors. In other words, the negative effects of dilution would be well worth it in the long-term.

There are other reasons that companies go public, too.

Sometimes the existing owners of a business want to sell their stock. Taking the company public is one way that they can do so.

An initial public offering (IPO) is when a private company sells new shares of stock to public investors. The shares are then traded on a public stock exchange such as the New York Stock Exchange or the NASDAQ Stock Exchange.

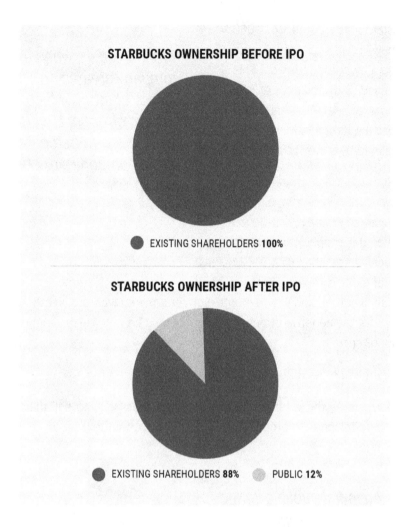

STARBUCKS OWNERSHIP BEFORE IPO

EXISTING SHAREHOLDERS **100%**

STARBUCKS OWNERSHIP AFTER IPO

EXISTING SHAREHOLDERS **88%**   PUBLIC **12%**

Sometimes companies go public simply because they want to make themselves more visible. When a company goes public, it often attracts a lot of media attention. That attention can help the business to acquire new customers.

However, the primary reason that companies go public is because they want to raise money.

COMPANIES CAN HAVE AS MANY SHARES AS THEY WANT

The total number of shares that a corporation has outstanding is a completely arbitrary number. It can also be changed at any time. The number of shares outstanding and the price of a single share do not tell you anything about the size or importance of a business.

Consider **NVR** (NYSE:NVR), which is a homebuilder in the U.S.. As of December 31, 2020, the company had a market capitalization of $15.1 billion, and yet it has chosen to only have 3.965 **million** shares outstanding. That's why a single share was worth $4,079.86 at the time.

By contrast, satellite radio giant **Sirius XM Holdings** (NYSE:SIRI) was worth about $25.6 billion as of December 31, 2020. That's $10 billion bigger than NVR. However, because Sirius has chosen to have 4.57 **billion** shares outstanding, its share price on the same date was only $6.37!

December 31, 2020	**NVR (NYSE:NVR)**	**Sirius XM Holdings (NASDAQ:SIRI)**
Market Capitalization	$15.1 billion	$26.6 billion
Shares outstanding	3,965,000	4,570,821,000
Share price	$4,079.86	$6.37

CHAPTER 9

DOES THE COMPANY GET THE MONEY WHEN AN INVESTOR BUYS THEIR STOCK?

In our example, Best Coffee Company went public so it could raise $100,000. It created 10,000 new shares of stock that were sold to public investors.

INITIAL PUBLIC OFFERING

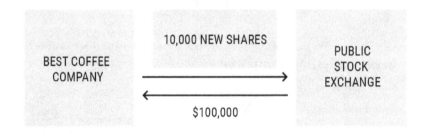

After those new shares were created and sold, *they no longer belong to Best Coffee Company.* They are owned by the investors who bought them on the public stock exchange.

The public investors who own those shares can choose to hold them or sell them.

In the event of a sale, *the investor who sold the stock gets the money,* not Best Coffee Company.

AFTER INITIAL PUBLIC OFFERING

CHAPTER 10

WHY DO INVESTORS BUY A COMPANY'S STOCK?

There's only one reason why investors buy stock: to make money. And there are two ways that investors can make money by owning stock.

The first way is to buy the stock for one price and then sell it at a higher price. This is possible when a stock goes up in value over time, which is called **appreciation**.

APPRECIATION

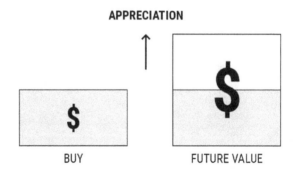

BUY   FUTURE VALUE

Let's use Best Coffee Company as an example. Alison buys stock in Best Coffee Company at the IPO for $10 per share. Brad doesn't buy at the IPO, but he wants to become a shareholder. He is willing to pay $15 for the stock. Alison sells her stock to Brad for $15.

Appreciation is when the value of an asset like a stock increases over time.

Alison bought the stock for $10 but sold it for $15. Alison earned $5 off of her $10 investment, which is a 50% return. This is called making money through a **capital gain**.

CAPITAL GAIN

$10	$5 CAPITAL GAIN
BUY	$10 $15
	SELL

The second way that investors can make money by owning stock is through dividends. As we covered in Chapter 3, a dividend is when a company chooses to give some of its profits back to its shareholders in the form of a cash payment.

Not all companies make dividend payments to their shareholders. Companies that choose to do so are called "**dividend stocks**."

Let's say that Best Coffee Company has a great year. It earns $20,000 in profits and decides to give all of that money to its shareholders by paying them a dividend.

How much of that $20,000 will each shareholder get?

To find out, we divide the total dividend payment by the total

A capital gain occurs when an asset is sold for a higher price than it was purchased.

43

number of shares.

$$\frac{\$20,000}{20,000} \begin{array}{l} \leftarrow \text{Total dividend payment} \\ \\ \leftarrow \text{Total number of shares} \end{array} = \$1.00 \text{ per share}$$

Then, we multiply the result by the number of shares that each holder owns:

	Natalie	Ethan	Lauren	Public Investors	Total
Shares Owned	6,000	3,000	1,000	10,000	20,000
Dividend Per Share	$1	$1	$1	$1	$1
Total Payment	$6,000	$3,000	$1,000	$10,000	$20,000

In some cases, investors can make money in a stock through both capital gains and dividends.

A dividend stock is a company that pays a dividend to its shareholders.

PART 2 REVIEW

- The primary reason why companies go public is because they want to raise money from investors by selling new shares of stock.

- Companies can also go public because they want to create an easy way for existing shareholders to sell their stock. Other times, they just want to make the company more visible to the public.

- Most companies go public through an Initial Public Offering (IPO).

- Companies only get money from selling stock when new stock is created and sold to investors.

- The downside of creating new stock is that existing shareholders are diluted.

- When a stock is sold by an investor, the investor gets the money from the sale, not the company.

- Investors buy stock because they want to make money.

- Investors make money by owning stock from appreciation and dividends.

- Appreciation is when a stock goes up in value over time.

- Some companies give a portion of their profits back to their investors in the form of dividends.

PART 3
VALUING A
BUSINESS

CHAPTER 11

HOW DO INVESTORS DETERMINE WHAT A BUSINESS IS WORTH?

Assume that Best Coffee Company makes exactly $20,000 in profits (which are also called "earnings") each year. That also equals $1.00 in earnings per share each year.

$$\frac{\$20,000 \quad \leftarrow \text{ Total earnings each year}}{20,000 \quad \leftarrow \text{ Total number of shares}} = \begin{array}{l} \$1.00 \text{ earnings} \\ \text{per share} \end{array}$$

Let's also assume that the company's earnings never change. Year in and year out, Best Coffee Company earns exactly $20,000 in profits.

Here's what Best Coffee Company's financials would look like over the next 10 years:

BEST COFFEE COMPANY					
Year	**1**	**2**	**3**	**4**	**5**
Stores	1	1	1	1	1
Earnings Per Year	$20,000	$20,000	$20,000	$20,000	$20,000
Total Shares Outstanding	20,000	20,000	20,000	20,000	20,000
Earnings Per Share	$1.00	$1.00	$1.00	$1.00	$1.00

Year	**6**	**7**	**8**	**9**	**10+**
Stores	1	1	1	1	1
Earnings Per Year	$20,000	$20,000	$20,000	$20,000	$20,000
Total Shares Outstanding	20,000	20,000	20,000	20,000	20,000
Earnings Per Share	$1.00	$1.00	$1.00	$1.00	$1.00

How much would you pay to own one share of Best Coffee Company?

Let's assume you are only willing to pay $2.00 for one share of stock. A Best Coffee Company shareholder agrees to this price and sells it to you for $2.00.

What is your return on investment? In other words, what is the annual rate of return on the $2 that you invested?

To find out, we divide the earnings per share by the price that you paid for one share.

$$\frac{\$1}{\$2} = 50\%$$

$\leftarrow$ Yearly earnings per share

$\leftarrow$ Price paid for one share

A 50% return on investment in one year is *really, really high*! After all, would you rather have your money invested in Best Coffee Company earning 50% per year or have it in a savings account at a bank earning 1% per year?

This means that $2 per share is a *wonderful* purchase price for the buyer. However, when a purchase price is a great deal for the buyer then it must also be a *terrible* price for the seller.

Let's take it to the other extreme.

Let's say that you are so desperate to own Best Coffee Company's stock that you are willing to pay $1,000 for one share. A shareholder agrees to this price and sells it to you.

What is your return on investment now?

$$\frac{\$1}{\$1,000} = 0.1\%$$

$\leftarrow$ Yearly earnings per share

$\leftarrow$ Price paid for one share

With just a 0.1% return on your investment, why would you even bother buying shares of Best Coffee Company? You could stick your money in a bank account and earn a 1% return, which is 10 times higher

This means that $1,000 per share is a *terrible* purchase price for the buyer. However, it also means that $1,000 is a *wonderful* price for the seller.

So, $2 per share is too low and $1,000 per share is too high.

How about $10 per share?

Here's how the return on investment looks at that purchase price.

$$\frac{\$1 \quad \leftarrow \text{ Earnings per share}}{\$10 \quad \leftarrow \text{ Price paid for one share}} = 10\%$$

A 10% return seems much more reasonable for both the buyer and the seller. The buyer earns a higher return than they could earn by keeping their money in a bank. The seller gets a decent price on the stock as well.

This—in an incredibly simple scenario—is how stocks are valued. The price is determined by a balancing act between buyers and sellers.

Buyers want as low of a price as possible so they can earn a high future return.

Sellers want as high of a price as possible so they can make the most money from their investment.

At any given time, investors determine what a business is worth based on two primary factors:

1. How much profit a company is expected to earn in the future.
2. How much investors are willing to pay to buy those earnings today.

CHAPTER 12

WHAT IS THE PRICE-TO-EARNINGS (P/E) RATIO?

In Chapter 11, we agreed that $10 per share was a fair price for Best Coffee Company.

The $10 per share price allowed the buyer to earn a 10% annual return on their investment.

$$\frac{\$1 \leftarrow \text{Earnings per share}}{\$10 \leftarrow \text{Price paid for one share}} = 10\%$$

Another way of saying this is that the buyer and seller agreed that $1 in earnings per share from Best Coffee Company is currently worth $10 in market value today.

There's a common term that investors use to describe this: the **price-to-earnings (P/E) ratio**.

Here's what this looks like for Best Coffee Company:

$$\frac{\$10 \leftarrow \text{Price per share}}{\$1 \leftarrow \text{Earnings per share}} = \text{P/E ratio of 10}$$

Investors would say that Best Coffee Company is currently valued at "10 times earnings." This is because its current P/E ratio is 10.

The P/E ratio is one of the most commonly used numbers by investors to figure out how much a company is currently worth.

The *lower* the P/E ratio is, the *cheaper* the company is to buy. The *higher* the P/E ratio, the more *expensive* a company is to buy.

The P/E ratio makes it easy for investors to compare opportunities to each other.

For example, if the P/E ratio of Best Coffee Company is 10 and the P/E ratio of Starbucks is 20, then you could argue that Best Coffee Company was a more attractive investment than Starbucks (holding all other factors equal). That's because Best Coffee Company's P/E ratio of 10 is much cheaper than Starbucks' P/E ratio of 20.

It can also be useful to compare a company's P/E ratio to a group of stocks, such as the S&P 500 Index.

If the P/E ratio of Best Coffee Company is 10 and the P/E ratio of the average stock in the S&P 500 was 20, then you could argue that Best Coffee Company was a better buy than the average company in the S&P 500.

To be clear, there are lots of ways that investors value businesses. The P/E ratio is just one of the most basic and widely used methods. The P/E ratio isn't useful for assessing the value of all stocks all the time. There are a lot of companies that the P/E ratio doesn't work on.

> *The price-to-earning (P/E) ratio simply divides the price per share by the earnings per share.*

For example, if a company is

growing rapidly but doesn't yet have any earnings, the P/E ratio won't be helpful. If a company is in an industry that is at risk of disappearing in five years, the P/E ratio won't be useful either.

However, the P/E ratio is a very useful number for investors to know.

CHAPTER 13

DOES GROWTH CHANGE A COMPANY'S VALUE?

In Chapter 11, we assumed that Best Coffee Company makes *exactly* $20,000 in profits (or "earnings") each year. That also equals $1.00 in earnings per share.

We determined that a P/E ratio of 10 for this business was fair for both the buyer and the seller. This means that in year 10, one share of the no-growth Best Coffee Company would be worth $10 per share. (See page 49 for more details).

EARNINGS PER SHARE IN YEAR 10	x	P/E RATIO	=	PRICE PER SHARE
$1	x	10	=	$10

But remember, Best Coffee Company went public because it wanted to build 10 new stores.

Let's assume that Best Coffee Company opens one new store per year. We'll also assume that each store produces exactly $20,000 in profits each year.

Here's what Best Coffee Company's financials would look like over the next 10 years:

OPEN ONE NEW STORE EACH YEAR EACH STORE EARNS $20,000 IN PROFITS					
Year	1	2	3	4	5
Stores	1	2	3	4	5
Earnings Per Year	$20,000	$40,000	$60,000	$80,000	$100,000
Total Shares	20,000	20,000	20,000	20,000	20,000
Earnings Per Share	$1.00	$2.00	$3.00	$4.00	$5.00

Year	6	7	8	9	10
Stores	6	7	8	9	10
Earnings Per Year	$120,000	$140,000	$160,000	$180,000	$200,000
Total Shares	20,000	20,000	20,000	20,000	20,000
Earnings Per Share	$6.00	$7.00	$8.00	$9.00	$10.00

If the P/E ratio of this version of Best Coffee Company was always fixed at 10, how much would one share of this company be worth in year 10? The answer is $100!

EARNINGS PER SHARE IN YEAR 10	X	P/E RATIO	=	PRICE PER SHARE
$10	X	10	=	$100

Which business would you rather own?

1. The no-growth business that makes the same amount of profit each year
2. The growing business that increases its profits each year

The company that is growing its profits each year! Why? Because the investor would earn a much higher return on their investment when buying the growing business.

Here's a harder question: If a fair P/E ratio for the no-growth business is 10, what is a fair P/E ratio for the business that is growing?

Would you be willing to pay *more* than 10 times earnings in year one for the growing business? You should! You would earn a much higher rate of return by owning the growing business, *even if you paid a higher P/E ratio for it*.

That's because businesses that are growing their profits have the ability to share a larger and larger stream of profits with their owners.

That means that investors should be willing to pay a higher P/E ratio for a company that is growing than one that is not.

PART 3 REVIEW

- The price of a stock is determined by how much profit a business is expected to make in the future and how much investors are willing to pay now to own those future profits.

- Buyers want as low of a price as possible so they can earn a high return. Sellers want as high of a price as possible.

- The price-to-earnings (P/E) ratio is found by dividing the price of a stock by its earnings per share.

- A business that is growing is worth more than a business that is not growing.

PART 4

WHY THE MARKET MOVES UP AND DOWN

CHAPTER 14

WHAT CAUSES THE P/E RATIO TO CHANGE?

In Chapter 12, we agreed that a 'fair' price-to-earnings (P/E) ratio for the no-growth Best Coffee Company that earned $20,000 each year was 10.

In the real world, the P/E ratio is not a fixed number. It changes all the time. Most of the time the changes in the P/E ratio are small. Every now and then these changes can be huge.

Let's imagine two different news stories to see why the P/E ratio might change.

HYPOTHETICAL NEWS STORY 1: Starbucks announces that it is going to build new stores right next door to every Best Coffee Company location.

This announcement would be bad news for Best Coffee Company. Some consumers might choose to buy coffee from Starbucks instead of Best Coffee Company. That would make it much less likely that Best Company Coffee would earn $20,000 in profits each year.

If you were about to invest in Best Coffee Company's stock and the Starbucks news broke, would you still be willing to pay 10 times earnings for that stock? The odds are good that you would not. This news would lower your belief in Best Coffee Company's ability to produce $20,000 in profits each year. It would make sense to demand a lower P/E ratio to offset this new risk.

How much lower of a P/E ratio would you demand? Let's say you are now only willing to pay 5 times earnings (a P/E ratio of 5).

In that case, the share price of Best Coffee Company *would get cut in half.*

	Before Starbucks Announcement		After Starbucks Announcement
P/E Ratio	10		5
Earnings Per Share	$1.00		$1.00
Share Price	$10.00	→	$5.00

By paying just 5 times earnings, the buyer would earn a 20% return on their investment. That might be a high enough return to justify the extra risk.

$$\frac{\$1 \leftarrow \text{Earnings per share}}{\$5 \leftarrow \begin{array}{l}\text{Price paid for one share}\\\text{at P/E of 5}\end{array}} = \begin{array}{l}20\% \text{ return}\\\text{on investment}\end{array}$$

In general, when bad news comes along, buyers are less willing to buy stocks. They demand a lower P/E ratio, which causes *the share price to fall.*

Now, let's consider what happens when good news comes along.

HYPOTHETICAL NEWS STORY 2: Best Coffee Company announces that it will start selling donuts.

Many customers like to buy donuts with their coffee. This announcement would be viewed as great news by Best Coffee Company's investors. Selling donuts would make it much more likely that Best Company Coffee will earn $20,000 in profits each year. It might even mean that the company's profits could grow.

If you were about to buy Best Coffee Company's stock, would you be willing to pay *more* than 10 times earnings? Odds are that you would.

How much more would the buyer be willing to pay? Let's say that you would now be willing to pay 20 times earnings (P/E ratio of 20) because you are so excited by the donut news.

In that case, the price of one share of Best Coffee Company *just doubled!*

	Before Donut Announcement		After Donut Announcement
P/E Ratio	10		20
Earnings Per Share	$1.00		$1.00
Share Price	$10.00	⟶	$20.00

By paying 20 times earnings, the buyer would be willing to accept just a 5% return on their investment now.

$$\frac{\$1}{\$20} \begin{array}{l} \leftarrow \text{Earnings per share} \\ \leftarrow \text{Price paid for one share} \\ \text{at P/E of 20} \end{array} = \begin{array}{l} 5\% \text{ return} \\ \text{on investment} \end{array}$$

However, Best Coffee Company now has the potential to earn much higher profits later. If that happened, the value of Best Coffee Company's stock would grow over time. That potential growth would make the buyer much more willing to pay a higher P/E ratio now.

In general, when good news comes along, investors are more eager to buy stocks. They are willing to pay a higher P/E ratio, which causes the *share price to rise*.

Importantly, in both theoretical examples, Best Coffee Company was the same business producing $20,000 in profits each year (or $1 in earnings per share).

However, news came along that **changed buyers' and sellers' perception** about the future profits of Best Coffee Company.

The P/E ratio—and the share price—moved up and down in response.

CHAPTER 15

WHY DOES A STOCK GO UP AND DOWN EVERY DAY?

In the last chapter, we saw how bad news could cause a company's share price to drop. We also saw how good news could cause a company's share price to rise.

What happens on days when there is no news? Most stocks still go up and down a little bit.

Why?

Sometimes, investors as a group feel a little bit more optimistic about a company's future. That optimism makes them willing to pay a slightly higher P/E ratio to own the stock. In turn, the stock price rises a little.

Other times, investors as a group feel a little bit more pessimistic about a company's future. That pessimism makes them demand a slightly lower P/E ratio to own the stock. This causes the stock price to fall a little.

Consider what happened to **Starbucks** (NASDAQ:SBUX) on Thursday, November 12, 2020. Starbucks didn't release any news on this particular day.

Starbucks started the trading day at $94.66. Over the course of the day, the stock dropped. It fell to $92.66, before ending the day at $93.54.

The small decline suggested that investors felt slightly more pessimistic about Starbucks' future at the end of the day than they did at the beginning of the day. The share price fell a little in response.

Importantly, **there was no news to explain why this happened.** For whatever reason, on Thursday, November 12, Starbucks investors felt slightly more pessimistic about the company's future. The stock fell in response.

The exact opposite situation happened *the very next day.*

On Friday, November 13, 2020, Starbucks didn't release any news. It started the trading day at $94.38, which was a little bit higher than it closed the day before. Over the course of the day, the stock rose. It rose to $95.59, and then ended the day at $95.30.

The stock price increase suggests that investors felt slightly more optimistic about Starbucks' future at the end of the day than they did at the beginning. The share price rose in response.

This is the most common reason why stocks move up and down each day. They move based on how investors as a group *feel* on any given day.

To understand why, it's helpful to think of the stock market as a live, on-going auction. Let's say that a stock is trading for $100. Some of its shareholders are in a foul mood and place an order to sell at any price over $100.10, which is the current market price. This is called the **ask price**, which is the lowest price that a seller will accept for a security.

Let's say that there are some investors who want to buy the stock, but are not willing to pay $100. They will only buy if the price is $99.90 or less. This is called the **bid price**, which is the highest price a buyer will pay for a security.

In this scenario, the ask price is $100.10 and the bid price is $99.90. The difference between those two numbers if $0.20. That is called the **spread**, which is the difference between the ask price and the bid price.

Let's say that some of the existing shareholders are more eager to sell than the potential buyers are to buy. One of the sellers decides to accept the $99.90 bid price. The transaction goes through and the stock price falls to $99.90, which is the last price that a trade took place.

In this case, the eagerness of the sellers outweighed the eagerness of the buyers, causing the stock price to fall.

The inverse can also be true. If potential buyers are more eager to buy than existing shareholders are to sell, the price *rises* to the point that existing shareholders are willing to sell.

Ask Price: *the lowest price that a seller will accept for a security.*

Bid Price: *the highest price a buyer will pay for a security.*

Spread: *the difference between the ask price and the bid price.*

Optimism causes prices to rise. Pessimism causes prices to fall.

Occasionally, news comes along that causes investors to feel a lot more optimistic or a lot more pessimistic than normal.

Consider what happened to Starbucks' stock on Friday, March 13, 2020—eight months earlier. Starbucks ended the trading day at $68.83 per share. However, large portions of the United States were shut down that following weekend because of COVID-19. That news caused investors to fear that Starbucks' profits were going to fall in the future. Starbucks' stock fell from $68.83 to $57.67 on Monday, March 17, 2020 in response to that fear.

The reverse is also true. Good news can cause a stock to rise rapidly.

On Tuesday, August 25, 2020, Starbucks announced that it would sell Pumpkin Spice Lattes and Salted Caramel Mocha Frappuccino earlier than usual. That news caused investors to believe that Starbucks profits were about to rise.

Starbucks' stock rose from $78.31 to $82.33 on Tuesday, August 25, 2020 in response.

In all cases, a stock price changes based on how investors as a group feel about the company at any given time.

That is why stocks rise or fall on any given day.

CHAPTER 16

WHY DOES THE STOCK MARKET GO UP AND DOWN EVERY DAY?

How investors *feel* impacts how a single stock price can fluctuate through the day. *The exact same thing happens to the stock market as a whole.*

The stock market has a P/E ratio that changes a little bit every day. The chart below shows the P/E ratio of the S&P 500 from January 1st, 2010 through January 1st, 2019:

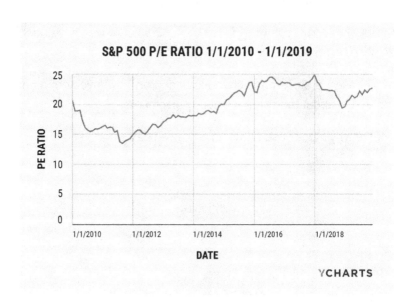

In January 2010, the P/E ratio of the S&P 500 was a little more than 20. The P/E ratio gradually fell over the next 20 months before it bottomed out around 13 in late 2011. From there it steadily expanded until it reached 25 in January 2018. Then it declined to 19.

None of those movements were in a straight line. The number bounced around.

In all cases, the P/E ratio changed slightly based on how investors as a group felt on any given day.

Sometimes, investors felt a little bit more optimistic about the future profits of all of the companies in the S&P 500. That optimism made them willing to pay a higher P/E ratio. In turn, stock prices rose.

Other times, investors felt a little bit more pessimistic about the future profits of the companies in the S&P 500. That pessimism made them demand a slightly lower P/E ratio to buy stocks. In turn, stock prices fell.

Every now and then, news comes along that causes the entire stock market to rise or fall a lot.

In early 2020, the COVID-19 pandemic was sweeping across the world. Businesses were forced to close. Social distancing orders were put into place. The unemployment rate skyrocketed.

Investors started to panic. That fear caused the S&P 500 to drop more than 25% between the middle of February and the middle of March.

On Friday, March 13, 2020, the U.S. Government announced that it would pass a bill to expand sick time leave and put money in Americans' pockets to help combat the financial hardship of the crisis. The S&P 500 rose 9% in a single day in response to the news.

That optimism proved to be short-lived. The situation got worse over the weekend. Investors panicked. On Monday, March 16, 2020, the S&P 500 fell 12% in a single day.

In all cases, **the stock market moved up or down based on how optimistic or pessimistic investors felt on any given day**.

WHY DOES A STOCK GO UP OR DOWN OVER THE LONG-TERM?

Let's pretend that Best Coffee Company is always valued at exactly 10 times earnings.

Let's also pretend that Best Coffee Company succeeds in opening up one new store each year. Each store creates $20,000 in new profits.

What would the price of one share of Best Coffee Company be in year one? The answer is $10.

Earnings Per Share $1	×	P/E Ratio 10	=	Price $10

What should the price of one share of Best Coffee Company be in year two? The answer is $20.

Earnings Per Share $2	×	P/E Ratio 10	=	Price $20

You can perform this calculation for every year to find the price.

OPEN 1 NEW STORE EACH YEAR EACH STORE EARNS $20,000 IN PROFITS				
Year	1	2	3	4	5
Stores	1	2	3	4	5
Total Earnings	$20,000	$40,000	$60,000	$80,000	$100,000
Total Shares	20,000	20,000	20,000	20,000	20,000
Earnings Per Share	$1.00	$2.00	$3.00	$4.00	$5.00
P/E Ratio	10	10	10	10	10
Price Per Share	$10.00	$20.00	$30.00	$40.00	$50.00

Year	6	7	8	9	10
Stores	6	7	8	9	10
Total Earnings	$120,000	$140,000	$160,000	$180,000	$200,000
Total Shares	20,000	20,000	20,000	20,000	20,000
Earnings Per Share	$6.00	$7.00	$8.00	$9.00	$10.00
P/E Ratio	10	10	10	10	10
Price Per Share	$60.00	$70.00	$80.00	$90.00	$100.00

The price of one share of Best Coffee Company went from $10 in year one to $100 in year 10. If you bought it in year one and held it until year 10, *you would have earned 10 times your initial investment!*

This is why a stock goes up over the long term. The share price follows changes in earnings.

When earnings go up, the stock price goes up.

When earnings go down, the stock price goes down.

Of course, in the real world, the P/E ratio is not a fixed number. It is constantly expanding and contracting based on how optimistic and pessimistic investors feel at any given time.

However, over the long-term, the price of a stock always follows the earnings of the company.

Starbucks' earnings increased from less than $0.01 per share in 1992 to $2.71 per share by 2019.

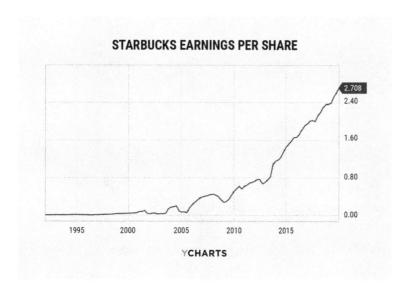

STARBUCKS EARNINGS PER SHARE

YCHARTS

* The earnings per share have been adjusted for one-time events that temporarily increased or decreased profits.

Starbucks' stock increased from $0.34 per share in 1992 to $64.40 per share by 2019.

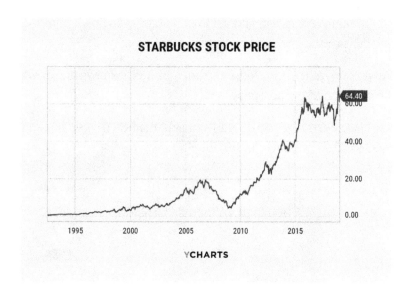

Here's what those two charts look like when they are put together.

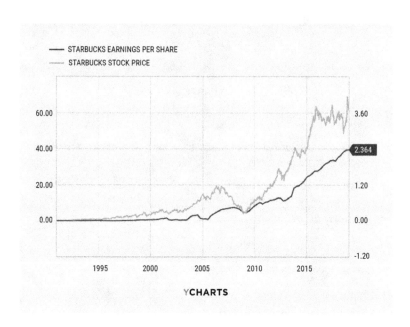

Sometimes Starbucks' share price went up faster than its profits. This happened because investors were feeling optimistic and Starbucks' P/E ratio expanded.

Other times Starbucks' share price went down even though its profits were rising. This happened because investors were feeling pessimistic and Starbucks' P/E ratio contracted.

In the short-term, a stock can move up or down for any number of reasons.

But over the long-term, prices move up and down based on changes in earnings.

Benjamin Graham, a famous investor, summed up this process beautifully:

> "In the short run, the market is like a voting machine—tallying up which firms are popular and unpopular. But in the long run, the market is like a weighing machine—assessing the substance of a company."

CHAPTER 18

WHY DOES THE STOCK MARKET GO UP OR DOWN OVER THE LONG-TERM?

The same force that moves a single company stock applies to the stock market as a whole.

This graph shows the historic earnings of the S&P 500.

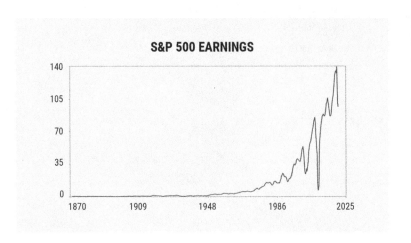

As you can see, the earnings of the S&P 500 have grown significantly over time (We will cover why earnings rise over time in Part 6).

In turn, the price of the S&P 500 has increased with it. From $4.44 in 1871 to $3,756 in 2020.

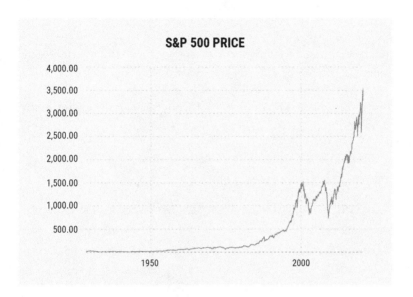

Here's what those two charts look like when they are put together.

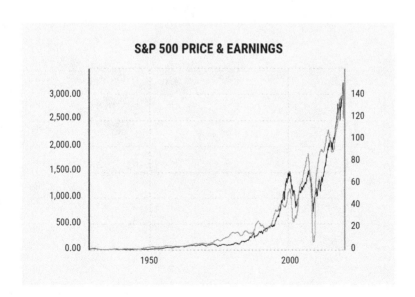

Sometimes the S&P 500's price went up faster than its profits. This happened because investors were feeling optimistic, and the P/E ratio expanded.

Sometimes the S&P 500's price went down even though its profits were rising. This happened because investors were feeling pessimistic, and the P/E ratio contracted.

In the short-term, the stock market can move up or down for any number of reasons.

In the long-term, the stock market moves up or down based on *changes in earnings.*

When earnings rise, the stock market rises. When earnings fall, the stock market falls.

CHAPTER 19

HOW OFTEN DOES THE STOCK MARKET GO UP?

You may have heard that the stock market goes up about 10% annually. That's true. But you'd never know it if you only look at daily stock price movements.

The odds that the S&P 500 will go up on any given day are slightly better than a coin flip. Stocks rise about 52% of the time and fall 48% of the time.

The odds improve when you look at the S&P 500 over a period of a month. The S&P 500 goes up 61% of the time and down 39% of the time.

Over a 6-month period, it goes up 66% of the time.

Over a 1-year period, it goes up 69% of the time.

Things get even more interesting when you look at even longer holding periods.

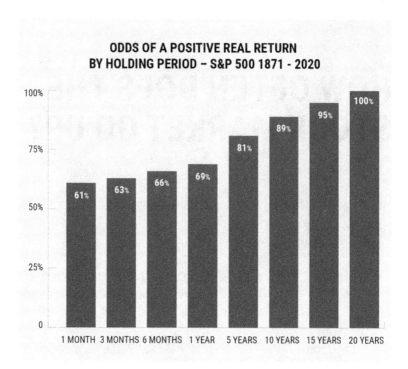

ODDS OF A POSITIVE REAL RETURN
BY HOLDING PERIOD – S&P 500 1871 - 2020

There are two important takeaways from this information:

1. As the holding period increases, the odds of achieving a positive return increase.
2. The S&P 500 has produced a positive return 100% of the time over every 20-year holding period.

That's pretty incredible when considering all of the bad stuff that has happened in U.S. history. The country has dealt with economic depressions, two world wars, pandemics, Presidential assassinations, high inflation, civil unrest, high unemployment, and terrorist attacks.

And yet, when stocks are held for a long enough time period, **they have delivered a positive return 100% of the time**.

PART 4 REVIEW

- The P/E ratio is not fixed; it changes all the time.

- When good news comes along, investors are more eager to buy stocks. They are willing to pay a higher P/E ratio and stock prices rise.

- When bad news comes along, investors are less willing to buy stocks. They demand a lower P/E ratio and stock prices fall.

- In the short-term, prices change based on how investors *feel* about a company.

- When investors feel slightly more optimistic, prices rise a little. When investors feel much more optimistic, prices rise a lot.

- When investors feel slightly more pessimistic, prices drop a little. When investors feel much more pessimistic, prices drop a lot.

- Over the long-term, prices move up and down based on changes in earnings.

- Over a 1-year period, the odds that the S&P 500 will rise are about 69%.

- As your holding period increases, your odds of making money increase.

- There has never been a 20-year period in U.S. history where the S&P 500 didn't produce a positive return.

PART 5

STOCK MARKET CRASHES AND RECOVERY

CHAPTER 20

WHY DOES THE STOCK MARKET CRASH?

Even though the S&P 500 goes up over the long term, there are still noticeable dips every so often.

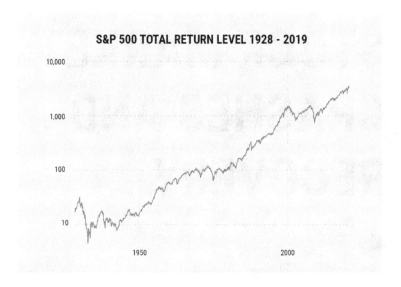

On a chart, the general trend is up and to the right, but the line isn't straight. There have been plenty of downturns along the way.

Every now and then the stock market experiences a big decline. When this happens, it is called a market "crash".

To find out why the market crashes, let's go back to our Best Coffee Company example.

Let's say that everything is going great for Best Coffee Company in its first three years. New stores are opening. Profits are growing. The stock price is going up.

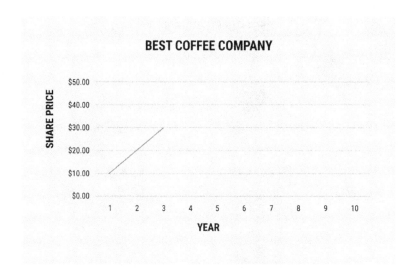

However, in the company's fourth year of expansion, a pandemic appears.

Consumers start to shop less often. Business activity slows to a crawl. Companies start to have a hard time paying their bills and lay off employees to save money.

Each day, fewer customers visit Best Coffee Company's stores.

If you were invested in Best Coffee Company and you saw this happening, how would you feel? You would likely be scared. You would probably think that Best Coffee Company's profits and stock price were about to fall.

Public investors would probably be afraid, too. Some of them would want to sell their stocks in order to get out ahead of a decline. That fear would make them willing to accept a lower stock price in order to sell quickly.

That sudden desire to sell at a lower price would cause the share price to drop.

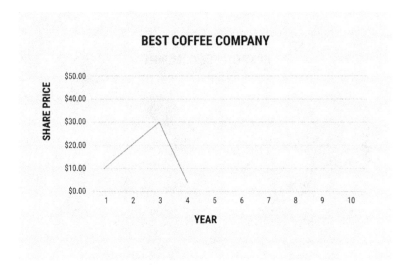

The declining share price would cause the price-to-earnings ratio to fall **in anticipation of a decline in earnings**.

Stock market crashes happen for the same reason.

Stock market crashes usually start when something bad happens in the world. That event causes investors to become worried that earnings are about to fall. That worry causes some investors to sell. That selling causes stock prices to fall, which causes even more investors to worry that stocks are going to fall.

That momentum feeds on itself until stock prices crash.

Historically, there have been a wide range of events that caused investors to fear that a market crash was coming. Wars, Presidential assassinations, changes in government policies, natural disasters, high inflation, terrorist attacks, too much debt, too much greed, financial crises, and more.

Here are the biggest stock market crashes in the S&P 500 over the last 100 years.

U.S. STOCK MARKET CRASHES				
What	**Start**	**End**	**Duration (Months)**	**S&P 500 Maximum Decline**
Great Depression	September 1929	June 1932	34	-86.10%
World War II Hangover	May 1946	June 1949	37	-29.60%
Bay of Pigs / Cuban Missile Crises	December 1961	June 1962	6	-28.00%
Inflation / Vietnam	November 1969	May 1970	18	-36.10%
Oil Embargo / Watergate	January 1973	October 1974	21	-48.00%
High Inflation / 20% Interest Rates	November 1980	August 1982	21	-27.80%
Black Monday	August 1987	December 1987	4	-34.00%
Dot-Com Crash	March 2000	October 2002	30	-59.10%
Housing Bubble/ Great Recession	October 2007	March 2009	17	-56.40%
COVID-19	February 2020	March 2020	1	-34.10%

In each case, the cause of the market crash was unique.

Some declines took years to recover from, such as the Great Depression and World War II. In other cases, the crash was finished in just a few months.

What's important to know is that stock market crashes are nothing new. They are a normal part of investing.

Since they are always caused by human emotions, they are also unpredictable. History shows that the stock market crashes every decade or so. The odds are good that it will continue to crash every decade or so into the future.

However, the stock market has also always recovered from the crash. We'll learn why in the next chapter.

CHAPTER 21

WHY HAS THE STOCK MARKET ALWAYS RECOVERED FROM CRASHES?

In Chapter 17, we learned that the stock market always follows earnings.

While the S&P 500 has always grown over time, earnings decline every now and then. We covered the various causes of those market crashes in the last chapter. However, despite all of the bad stuff that has happened, earnings have always recovered and gone on to reach new highs.

To see why, let's continue with our Best Coffee Company example from Chapter 20.

In Best Coffee Company's fourth year a pandemic occurred. Some of Best Coffee Company's investors became worried that earnings were about to fall. They sold the stock in order to sidestep the decline. Let's say that the pandemic was so bad that the earnings at each of Best Coffee Company's stores fell from $20,000 per store to just $2,000 per year.

How far would Best Coffee Company's stock fall if the P/E ratio still held steady at 10?

Year	1	2	3	4
Stores	1	2	3	4
Earnings Per Store	$20,000	$20,000	$20,000	$2,000
Earnings Per Year	$20,000	$40,000	$60,000	$8,000
Total Shares	20,000	20,000	20,000	20,000
Earnings Per Share	$1.00	$2.00	$3.00	$0.40
P/E Ratio	10	10	10	10
Price Per Share	$10.00	$20.00	$30.00	$4.00

The price per share would fall from $30 in year three all the way down to $4 per share in year four. That's a drop of over 85%!

If you were invested in Best Coffee Company, how would you feel if you saw the stock fall that much? You would probably be filled with fear. The value of your investment dropped by more than 85% in a single year!

Remember Best Coffee Company's owners Natalie, Ethan, and Lauren? Their investment would have dropped as well. How do you think they would respond to such a huge decline in profits?

They would probably make some drastic changes to get the company's profits back up.

What changes could they make? Here are a few ideas:

■ Create a website to enable customers to order Best Coffee Company from home.

■ Start selling bagels, muffins, shakes, donuts, and candy at the stores to create new revenue opportunities.

■ Open the stores earlier each day and close them later.

■ Negotiate with their suppliers to lower costs.

The huge profit decline would force Natalie, Ethan, and Lauren to try new business practices. It's likely that some of these actions would help to reverse the big decline in earnings.

What's more, the pandemic wouldn't just affect Best Coffee Company. It would also impact Best Coffee Company's competitors. Some of them could go out of business in the downturn. Their customers might choose to buy from Best Coffee Company instead.

Importantly, these moves would probably make Best Coffee Company a much stronger company in the future.

Let's say that by year 5 the worst of the pandemic is over. Best Coffee Company's profits recover to $10,000 per store.

By year 6, Best Coffee Company is back to earning $20,000 in profits per store.

By year 7, all of the changes that were made during the pandemic grew Best Coffee Company's profits per store all the way to $30,000.

Here's what Best Coffee Company's financial results over the 10-year period would look like:

OPEN 1 NEW STORE EACH YEAR DOWNTURN YEAR 4 / RECOVERY YEAR 6					
Year	1	2	3	4	5
Stores	1	2	3	4	5
Earnings Per Store	$20,000	$20,000	$20,000	$2,000	$10,000
Earnings Per Year	$20,000	$40,000	$60,000	$8,000	$50,000
Total Shares	20,000	20,000	20,000	20,000	20,000
Earnings Per Share	$1.00	$2.00	$3.00	$0.40	$2.50
P/E Ratio	10	10	10	10	10
Price Per Share	$10.00	$20.00	$30.00	$4.00	$25.00

Year	6	7	8	9	10
Stores	6	7	8	9	10
Earnings Per Store	$20,000	$30,000	$30,000	$30,000	$30,000
Earnings Per Year	$120,000	$210,000	$240,000	$270,000	$300,000
Total Shares	20,000	20,000	20,000	20,000	20,000
Earnings Per Share	$6.00	$10.50	$12.00	$13.50	$15.00
P/E Ratio	10	10	10	10	10
Price Per Share	$60.00	$105.00	$120.00	$135.00	$150.00

Here's what would happen to Best Coffee Company's stock if the P/E ratio held steady at 10 the entire way.

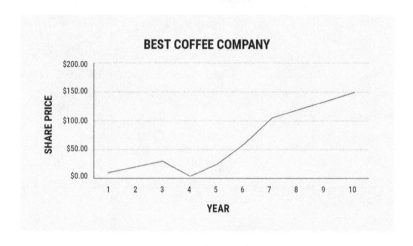

This is an overly simplified example, but it shows how a company can recover from a downturn and emerge stronger on the other side. The stock market works in a similar way. It has always recovered from past downturns and emerged stronger on the other side.

Here are three big reasons why:

First, tough times force companies, workers, and entrepreneurs to try new things. They abandon old business practices and adopt new ones. They begin to experiment with new technologies.

Consider what happened in 1873. The U.S. was in a depression. Yet in the following decade new innovations like the phonograph, light bulb, subway system, and telephone were all invented.

Or consider the Great Depression. The 1930s were one of the toughest economic periods in American history. Yet economic historian Alexander Field called it the most "technologically progressive decade of the 20th century."

In 2020, the COVID-19 pandemic caused millions of businesses to shut down. Video conferencing, work from home, and e-commerce became the norm. Companies that adapted to meet the new needs of the market not only survived, but they set themselves up for long-term success.

When tough times hit, businesses are forced to innovate and try new things. That innovation leads to new business formation. That leads to a recovery.

Second, weak businesses go belly-up in tough times, but strong businesses survive. The strong businesses eventually capture the customers of businesses that failed. That allows them to emerge stronger than ever before.

Third, the government steps in to provide assistance during downturns. This includes providing employment opportunities, direct payments, or buying goods and services from businesses. That can help to cushion the economic blow.

These three factors combined eventually end the downturn. The businesses that survive emerge stronger than ever. Profits eventually fully recover.

New businesses also start to pop up and grow quickly in a recovery. The new innovations and technologies they bring to market drive the economy. Eventually, investors recognize that earnings are recovering, which reinflates stock prices.

In other words, as long as business profits eventually recover from a downturn, the stock market will too.

PART 5 REVIEW

- Every decade or so the stock market experiences a big decline. When this happens, it is called a market "crash".

- Investors sell stocks in anticipation of a decline in earnings.

- Stock market crashes are nothing new. They are a normal part of investing.

- Stock market crashes are unpredictable because they are caused by human emotions.

- Tough economic times force businesses, workers, and entrepreneurs to try new things.

- Weak businesses die in downturns, which allows their stronger competitors to capture their customers.

- The government can assist in a downturn by putting people to work and buying goods and services. That can help to cushion the blow.

PART 6
WHY EARNINGS GO UP

CHAPTER 22

WHY DO EARNINGS GO UP?

As we've discussed in the past few chapters, the earnings of the S&P 500 have continued to grow over time, although not in a straight line. Every now and then the economy hits a rough patch and the earnings of the S&P 500 fall. However, the S&P 500's earnings have always recovered and eventually reached new highs.

There are several forces that work together to drive earnings up over time.

Those forces are:

1. Inflation
2. Productivity
3. Innovation
4. International expansion
5. Population growth
6. Acquisitions
7. Stock buybacks

Each of these forces usually has a small impact on earnings in any given year—maybe 1% or 2%. They also matter more in some years than in others. However, when they are combined, they consistently cause earnings to go up.

As long as all of these forces remain in place, **it is a near certainty that profits will continue to rise over time.**

CHAPTER 23

WHAT IS INFLATION?

McDonald's launched the Big Mac in 1967. The burger consisted of two beef patties, three buns, one slice of cheese, pickles, lettuce, onions, and a special sauce. It was priced at $0.45 and was an instant success. By 2020, the Big Mac had all of the same basic ingredients that it did in 1967. But now it costs about $5.

Why did the price go up so much? The answer is **inflation**.

You've probably noticed that the price of almost everything you buy—cars, food, houses, gasoline, insurance, health care—is higher today than when you were a kid.

Inflation occurs because money slowly loses its buying power over time. Businesses raise their prices a little bit each year to offset the loss of buying power. This causes their profits to increase a little bit each year, too.

Inflation is when the price of goods and services rise over time.

Believe it or not, inflation happens on purpose. The **Federal Reserve** aims to keep the inflation rate in the U.S. around 2% per year. To achieve this, the Federal Reserve steadily raises the total supply of money in the U.S.

The Federal Reserve, or simply "the Fed", is the central bank of the United States. The Fed was created by the U.S. Government to provide the nation with a more stable monetary and financial system. (See Chapter 59 for more details).

By increasing the total supply of money, the value of all dollars slowly decreases. That's because the more of something there is, the less valuable it becomes.

Think of it this way: A 1914 Babe Ruth rookie baseball card is extremely rare and highly desired by collectors. That scarcity makes it very valuable. One of these cards sold at auction in 2013 for $450,300.

What do you think would happen to the price of the exact same card if 10,000 mint condition 1914 Babe Ruth rookie baseball cards were suddenly discovered? The supply increase would cause the price to plunge. The higher the supply, the less valuable each individual baseball card becomes.

Money works the same way.

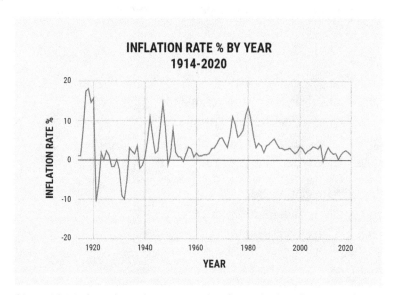

Since 1914, there have been periods of very high inflation and very low inflation. Over the last 30 years, the inflation rate has been modest.

But, over time, the inflation rate is likely to remain in positive territory. That will act as a force that increases business profits.

As long as the inflation rate remains above 0%, it will have a positive impact on earnings.

The Federal Reserve, or simply "the Fed", is the central bank of the United States.

CHAPTER 24

WHAT IS PRODUCTIVITY?

In 1950, an acre of planted corn produced 39 bushels per year. In 2000, the same acre of planted corn produced 153 bushels, an increase of 292%.

Corn wasn't an anomaly. Humans get much better at producing almost everything—dairy, energy, cars, light, electronics—over time.

There's a fancy name for getting better at making stuff: **productivity**.

Productivity gains come from many different sources. Building new factories, buying better equipment, sourcing cheaper materials, inventing new technologies, and developing new techniques all contribute to productivity.

In any given year, most productivity gains are barely noticeable. A little bit here, a little bit there. Over time, those productivity gains stack on top of each other and really add up.

Productivity means that humans find new ways to produce more goods and services with the same (or fewer) inputs.

The U.S. Government keeps track of productivity. It has been on an upward trend since 1950.

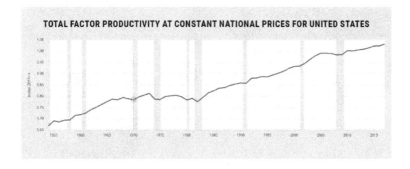

There have been ups and downs, but the long term trend is clear: productivity consistently goes up.

That's wonderful news for humanity. Improved productivity allows businesses to produce goods and services more efficiently. This can allow them to either increase their margins or pass on their savings to consumers.

That steadily grows their profits over time.

CHAPTER 25

WHAT IS INNOVATION?

In 1990, smartphones didn't exist. By 2020, more than 3 billion consumers had smartphones and annual smartphone sales totaled $700 billion.

Humans invent new technologies all the time. Every now and then those new technologies open up new market opportunities that didn't exist before. This is called **innovation**.

Whenever innovative technologies are created they open up new market opportunities for businesses. New and old companies compete against each other to create products and services that meet the new demand. As that demand is met, profits rise.

Innovation is when new types of goods and services are brought to market that open new opportunities for businesses.

Some innovations destroy older markets. When automobiles became the dominant form of transportation the demand for horses fell dramatically. However, the net effect of innovation usually leads to growth in profits.

What innovations are on the horizon? Here's a list of up-and-coming technologies that hold promise to open up new market opportunities:

- 5G
- 3D Printing
- Aquaculture
- Alternative Cement
- Artificial Intelligence
- Autonomous Vehicles
- Bioplastics
- Biotechnology
- Blockchain
- Brain-Machine Interfaces
- Carbon Sequestration
- Cloud Computing
- Connected Fitness
- Controlled Environment Agriculture
- CRISPR
- Cryptocurrencies
- Cybersecurity
- DNA Computing
- Desalination
- Digital Wallets
- Distributed Utilities
- Dynamic Glass
- Edge Computing
- Electric Bikes
- Electronic Payments
- Electronic Sports
- Electric Vehicles

- Energy Storage
- Fuel Cells
- Geothermal Heating & Cooling
- Gene Editing
- Holograms
- Hyperloop
- Internet-of-Things
- Longevity
- mRNA
- Metaverse
- Microgrid
- Nanotechnology
- Nuclear 2.0
- Online Dating
- Online Learning
- Personalized Medicine
- Personalized Insurance
- Plant-Based Dairy
- Plant-Based Meat
- Plastics 2.0
- Precision Biology
- Quantum Computing
- Real Estate iBuying
- Recycling 2.0
- Robotics
- Robotic Surgery
- Software-as-a-Service

- Smart Roads
- Solar Energy
- Solar Roofs
- Space Mining
- Space Tourism
- Streaming Video
- Telehealth
- Telepresence
- Tunneling 2.0
- Vertical Farming
- Waste Recycling
- Waste-to-Energy
- Virtual Reality
- Wireless Charging
- Wind Energy

CHAPTER 26

WHAT IS INTERNATIONAL EXPANSION?

Netflix was founded in 1997. The company's innovative idea was to rent DVDs through the mail instead of through retail stores. Netflix gradually caught on and was used by millions of Americans.

By 2010, Netflix began to transform itself from a DVD rental company into a digital streaming service. That change allowed the company to expand into other parts of the world like Canada, Latin America, and the Caribbean.

At the end of 2020, Netflix had more than 200 million global subscribers. More than half of them lived outside the United States.

Netflix is far from an anomaly. Lots of American companies—like Nike, Domino's, Apple, and McDonald's—generate most of their revenue outside of the U.S.

There were 7.8 billion humans on the planet as of 2020. Only 332 million of them lived in the United States. Companies are smart to increase their customer base outside of one country.

While the United States' economy is the largest and most developed in the world, lots of other countries are catching up. Large countries like China, India, Brazil, and Indonesia are growing their economies quickly. That's lifting billions of people out of poverty and is creating a global middle class.

American businesses are aware that foreign markets hold huge potential, so they continually search for ways to sell products and services to those new consumers. As they succeed, their profits grow.

WHAT IS POPULATION GROWTH?

In 1900 there were 1.6 billion humans on the planet.

By 2020, the total grew to 7.8 billion people.

By 2100, the United Nations estimates that this figure will reach 10.8 billion.

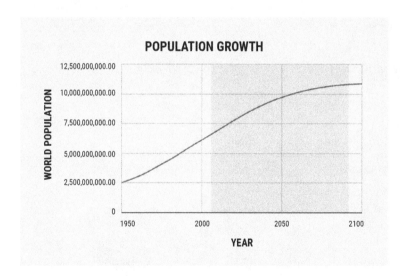

The slow increase in the world's population gradually increases the demand for all goods and services.

As businesses fill that higher demand, their profits increase.

CHAPTER 28

WHAT ARE ACQUISITIONS?

In Chapter 17, Best Coffee Company decided to use its profits to open up one new store each year.

> *An acquisition is when one company buys the majority of another company's stock in order to gain control of it.*

Opening up a store from scratch is hard. Natalie, Ethan, and Lauren have to find a location, build the store, hire employees, get supplies, and fill out lots of paperwork. It's a lot of work.

Wouldn't it be great if Best Coffee Company could just buy a rival coffee shop and rename it instead?

There's a fancy name for when a business buys another business: **an acquisition**.

When one company (the acquirer) buys another company (the acquiree), the acquirer gets to count all of the acquiree's revenue and profits as its own. This grows the acquirer's revenue and profits.

Aside from the financial benefits, there are lots of reasons why one company will buy another:

- To gain control of its assets

- To increase market share

- To lower costs

- To decrease competition

- To gain access to a new technology

- To add employees

- To enter a new market

- To diversify the number of products that are available for sale

For example, Amazon acquired the upscale grocery chain Whole Foods in 2017 for $13.4 billion. The acquisition instantly provided Amazon with hundreds of physical stores that it could use to sell groceries and other goods across the country.

Acquisitions have become very common. In 2020, American businesses spent more than $2.4 trillion to acquire more than 15,000 companies.

The number and size of acquisitions has grown over time.

Since acquisitions are a reliable way for companies to grow their revenue and profits, they will likely remain a popular way for companies to grow.

CHAPTER 29

WHAT ARE STOCK BUYBACKS?

As you will recall from Chapter 8, after Best Coffee Company went public each of the owners, Natalie, Ethan, and Lauren, had their ownership position cut in half. Natalie owned 30%, Ethan 15%, Lauren 5%, and the remaining 50% was divided among the public investors who purchased stock.

	Natalie	Ethan	Lauren	Public Investors	Total
Shares Owned	6,000	3,000	1,000	10,000	20,000
Ownership Percentage	30%	15%	5%	50%	100%

There are 20,000 shares in total. This means that Natalie, Ethan, and Lauren own half of Best Coffee Company. Public investors own the other half.

If you were Natalie, Ethan, and Lauren, wouldn't you want to have more control of the company? If they did, then Natalie, Ethan, and Lauren would have a larger claim on the company's profits and assets.

There is a way that Natalie, Ethan, and Lauren can do this. They need to reduce the number of shares that public investors own. This can be done with **stock buybacks**.

Some companies choose to use a portion of their profits to buy their stock "back" from their investors. When this happens, the total

number of shares that
exist declines. This leaves
all remaining shares with a
slightly larger piece of the
business.

A stock buyback is when a company repurchases shares of its stock from its investors.

Let's say that Natalie,
Ethan, and Lauren decided
to use some of their profits
to buy back 5,000 shares of stock from public investors.

Before the buyback there were 20,000 shares in total. After the buyback there are only 15,000 shares in total. This means that each remaining share has a larger claim on Best Coffee Company's profits. This makes each share more valuable.

After completing the buyback, Natalie still owns 6,000 shares of stock, so her ownership position in the company would rise from 30% to 40%. Ethan still owns 3,000 shares of stock, so his ownership position in the company would rise from 15% to 20%. Lauren still owns 1,000 shares of stock, so her ownership position in the company would rise from 5% to 7%.

	Natalie	Ethan	Lauren	Public Investors	Total
Shares Owned	6,000	3,000	1,000	5,000	15,000
Ownership Percentage	40%	20%	7%	33%	100%

Here's what the difference looks like in a pie chart.

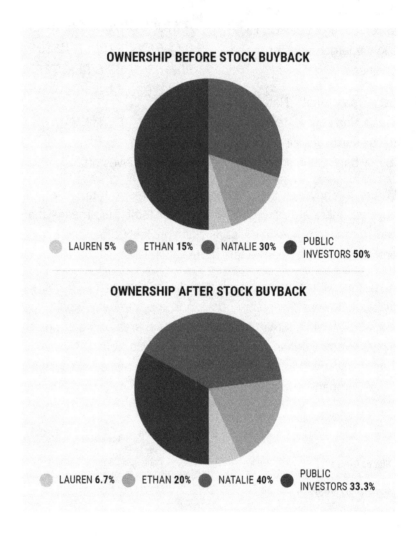

OWNERSHIP BEFORE STOCK BUYBACK

LAUREN 5%   ETHAN 15%   NATALIE 30%   PUBLIC INVESTORS 50%

OWNERSHIP AFTER STOCK BUYBACK

LAUREN 6.7%   ETHAN 20%   NATALIE 40%   PUBLIC INVESTORS 33.3%

The same principle works with the stock market as a whole.

Each year, companies in the S&P 500 spend billions of dollars to buy back their stock from investors.

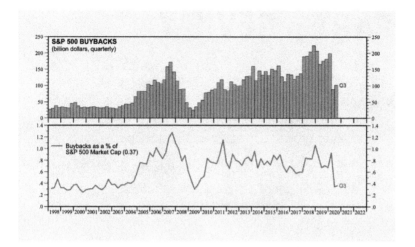

This reduces the total number of shares outstanding. In turn, the earnings per share increases because the total number of shares go down.

In any given year, stock buybacks don't amount to much. They grow earnings by 1% or so. However, when added up over time, they consistently lead to growth in earnings on a per share basis.

PART 6 REVIEW

- Earnings go up over time because of the combination of inflation, productivity, innovation, international expansion, population growth, acquisitions, and stock buybacks.

- Inflation is when the price of goods and services rises over time.

- Productivity is when humans find new ways to produce more goods and services with fewer inputs.

- Innovation is the introduction of new types of goods and services that open new market opportunities.

- International expansion is when companies sell their products and services in other countries.

- As the population continues to grow, demand for goods and services also grows.

- Acquisitions are when one company buys another company.

- A stock buyback is when a company repurchases its own shares from its investors.

PART 7

ALL ABOUT COMPOUNDING

CHAPTER 30

WHAT IS COMPOUNDING?

In Chapter 1, a fictional person named Aaron turned $400 per month into $3 million by investing in the market for 39 years.

What force allowed the account to grow to such a big number? The answer is **compounding**.

As Benjamin Franklin once said, "Money makes money. And the money that money makes, makes money."

Think of compounding like a snowball that is rolling down a big hill. The snowball starts small but gets larger as it travels down the hill. As it grows, the amount of snow that it picks up grows too. This allows the snowball to get bigger at a faster and faster rate.

To see how powerful compounding can be, consider this question:

If you doubled $1 thirty times, how much money would you have?

Compounding occurs when the proceeds from an investment are reinvested over and over again to generate additional returns. This causes the investment to get bigger at a faster and faster rate over time.

Answer: $1,073,741,824

Seems impossible, doesn't it?

Here's the math:

Doubling	Value	Doubling	Value	Doubling	Value
1	$2	11	$2,048	21	$2,097,152
2	$4	12	$4,096	22	$4,194,304
3	$8	13	$8,192	23	$8,388,608
4	$16	14	$16,384	24	$16,777,216
5	$32	15	$32,768	25	$33,554,432
6	$64	16	$65,536	26	$67,108,864
7	$128	17	$131,072	27	$134,217,728
8	$256	18	$262,144	28	$268,435,456
9	$512	19	$524,288	29	$536,870,912
10	$1,024	20	$1,048,576	30	$1,073,741,824

Here's what this looks like graphically.

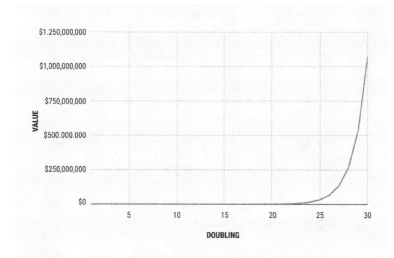

This incredible growth is made possible thanks to the power of compounding.

What makes the stock market so powerful is that it compounds an investor's money over time.

The key part of that last sentence is "over time". The secret to earning huge returns is to invest your money for as long as possible.

For example, if you invested $100 in the S&P 500 each month, how much would you have as of the end of 2020?

- If you started in 2010, you'd have $31,177.
- If you started in 2000, you'd have $85,046.
- If you started in 1990, you'd have $229,953.
- If you started in 1980, you'd have $864,666.
- If you started in 1970, you'd have $2,618,060.

Here is what these totals look like dating back to January of 1920:

VALUE OF $100 PER MONTH INVESTED IN THE S&P 500 AS OF DECEMBER 31, 2020

Starting Date	Value	Starting Date	Value
January 2010	$31,177	January 1960	$5,718,341
January 2000	$85,046	January 1950	$17,310,217
January 1990	$229,953	January 1940	$65,959,992
January 1980	$864,666	January 1930	$157,054,643
January 1970	$2,618,060	January 1920	$319,680,111

Notice how the total value is getting bigger at a faster and faster rate. That's compounding in action.

To understand why this happens, let's go back to Best Coffee Company.

Each new Best Coffee Company location costs $10,000 to build. The company's original plan was to raise $100,000 from public investors and open one new store each year.

Let's say that Natalie, Ethan, and Lauren decide to scrap that plan. Instead, they decide to open up new stores by reinvesting all of the company's annual profits to build as many stores as possible.

In year one, Best Coffee Company earned $20,000 in profits. Natalie, Ethan, and Lauren use this money to open two new stores the following year.

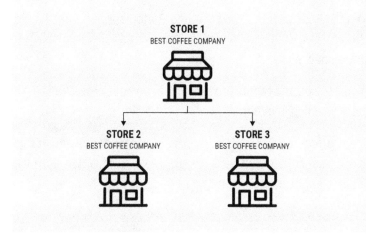

In year 2, Best Coffee Company has 3 stores open. This provides it with $60,000 in yearly profits. Natalie, Ethan, and Lauren open up **six** new stores with the profits the following year.

In year 3, Best Coffee Company has 9 stores open. That would allow it to earn $180,000 in profits. That would allow it to open up **eighteen** new stores the next year.

As you can see, the profits are growing at an accelerated rate. This is compounding in action.

If Best Coffee Company could keep its store count growing at this rate, by year 10 it would have 19,683 stores and would produce $393,660,000 in annual profits!

This is just an example, but it does showcase just how powerful compounding can be.

CHAPTER 31

HOW DOES THE STOCK MARKET COMPOUND?

Over the long-term, the S&P 500 has compounded at a rate of about 10% annually.

While there have been dips because of the market crashes that we discussed in Chapter 20, the compounding effect has still allowed the entire market to grow at relatively a consistent rate.

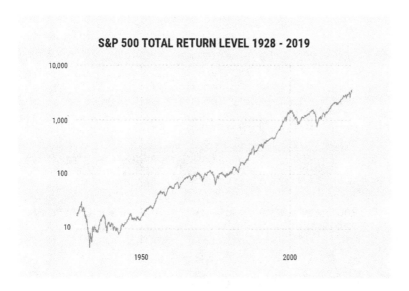

S&P 500 TOTAL RETURN LEVEL 1928 - 2019

When I first saw a long-term graph of the S&P 500, I became confused. All I saw was a line with a number on it gradually going up and to the right. How did this translate into a compound annual growth rate of 10% annually?

It was only later that I discovered the answer. Compounding occurs in the stock market because price movements are tracked in *percentages*, not points.

Have you ever heard a news reporter say something like "the Dow Jones Industrial Average rose 300 points today to 30,300?" What they are reporting is accurate; in this case the value of the Dow Jones Industrial Average increased by 300 points on this particular day. However, *you need to look at percentages to put the gain in context.*

A better way to say this would be "the Dow Jones Industrial Average rose 1% today." (The Dow rose 300 points divided by the previous day's closing price of 30,000 equals a 1% gain). This means that if you had $10,000 invested in the Dow Jones Industrial Average that it would now be worth $10,100 (a 1% increase).

Points provide facts. Percentages provide context.

What's more, the percentage movement in the index is reset on January 1st each year. All of the gains or losses that are recorded the following year use the level on January 1st as a starting point.

To showcase why, let's create a brand new index from scratch. The starting value on January 1st is exactly 100.

At the end of the year, the index rises to 110. That's a 10% increase.

$$\frac{110}{100} \quad \begin{array}{l} \longleftarrow \text{Ending Value on Dec. 31} \\ \longleftarrow \text{Staring Value on Jan. 1} \end{array} \quad = 110\% - 1 = 10\% \text{ increase}$$

On January 1st of the second year, the new denominator is 110.

Let's say the index rises another 10% in year 2. What's the value at the end of year 2?

It's 121!

That 10 that was earned in year 1 also grew 10%. That added an extra 1 to the total.

Let's assume that 10% returns continue for a few years.

By the end of year 10, the index grew from 100 all the way to 259!

Year	Starting Value	Gain	Ending Value
1	100	10%	110
2	110	10%	121
3	121	10%	133
4	133	10%	146
5	146	10%	161
6	161	10%	177
7	177	10%	195
8	195	10%	214
9	214	10%	236
10	236	10%	259

The Dow Jones Industrial Average, S&P 500, NASDAQ Composite all work the same way.

Here's the annual returns of the S&P 500 dating back to 1926.

\multicolumn{8}{c}{**S&P 500 RETURN BY YEAR**}
Year	% Change	Year	% Change	Year	% Change	Year	% Change
1926	11.62	1950	31.71	1974	(26.47)	1998	28.58
1927	37.49	1951	24.02	1975	37.20	1999	21.04
1928	43.61	1952	18.37	1976	23.84	2000	(9.10)
1929	(8.42)	1953	(0.99)	1977	(7.18)	2001	(11.89)
1930	(24.90)	1954	52.62	1978	6.56	2002	(22.10)
1931	(43.34)	1955	31.56	1979	18.44	2003	28.68
1932	(8.19)	1956	6.56	1980	32.42	2004	10.88
1933	53.99	1957	(10.78)	1981	(4.91)	2005	4.91
1934	(1.44)	1958	43.36	1982	21.55	2006	15.79
1935	47.67	1959	11.96	1983	22.56	2007	5.49
1936	33.92	1960	0.47	1984	6.27	2008	(37.00)
1937	(35.03)	1961	26.89	1985	31.73	2009	26.46
1938	31.12	1962	(8.73)	1986	18.67	2010	15.06
1939	(0.41)	1963	22.80	1987	5.25	2011	2.11
1940	(9.78)	1964	16.48	1988	16.61	2012	16.00
1941	(11.59)	1965	12.45	1989	31.69	2013	32.39
1942	20.34	1966	(10.06)	1990	(3.10)	2014	13.69
1943	25.90	1967	23.98	1991	30.47	2015	1.38
1944	19.75	1968	11.06	1992	7.62	2016	11.96
1945	36.44	1969	(8.50)	1993	10.08	2017	21.83
1946	(8.07)	1970	4.01	1994	1.32	2018	(4.38)
1947	5.71	1971	14.31	1995	37.58	2019	31.49
1948	5.50	1972	18.98	1996	22.96	2020	17.28
1949	18.79	1973	(14.66)	1997	33.36		

The S&P 500 market almost never returns 10% in any given year. The annual returns are all over the map.

Sometimes the S&P 500 is up big, like it was in 1928 when it rose 43% or 1954 when it rose 52%.

Sometimes the S&P 500 is down big, like it was in 1931 when it dropped 43% or 2008 when it fell 37%.

However, if you average out all of those wild swings over long periods of time, it rounds to an annual return of about 10%.

CHAPTER 32

DO DIVIDENDS PLAY A ROLE IN STOCK MARKET COMPOUNDING?

Over the long-term, the S&P 500 has compounded at a rate of about 10% annually.

Most of that return is driven by growth in the S&P 500's earnings. However, a portion of that 10% return is due to **dividend reinvestment**.

Investors have two choices when they receive a dividend payment:

1. They can take the dividend as cash
2. They can reinvest the dividend back into the stock or fund to buy more shares

Many investors choose to reinvest their dividends. That can be a smart move because dividend reinvestment can boost the stock or fund's long-term returns. That's because the dividends are used to buy more shares of the stock or fund, which increases the number of shares that the investor owns, which increases the size of future dividend payments, and so on.

As the dividends are reinvested, the investor's portfolio grows at a faster and faster rate.

How much of the investor's return comes from dividend reinvestment at any given time depends on the stock or fund's **dividend yield**.

Dividend yield is similar to an interest rate and is always displayed as a percentage. For example, the dividend yield on the S&P 500 at the end of 2020 was 1.5%. This means that if you invested $1,000 into the S&P 500 at that time then you would expect to receive $15 in dividend payments over the following year.

A 1.5% return might not sound like much, but dividend reinvestment can have a bigger impact on long-term returns than you might think.

Remember Aaron from Chapter 1? He turned a $400 per month investment into a $3.03 million portfolio over 39 years thanks to dividend reinvestment.

Aaron's investment portfolio grew at a compound annual growth rate of 11% during his career. However, only 8.5% of that total came from capital appreciation. The remaining 2.5% came from reinvesting dividends.

Believe it or not, that 2.5% made a *big* difference in the size of Aaron's portfolio.

Recall that Aaron's portfolio grew to $3,013,537 million with dividend reinvestment. How much would his portfolio be worth if he spent instead of reinvested his dividends?

$1,483,731

You read that right; if Aaron chose to spend his dividends

Dividend reinvestment is when the dividends that are received from a stock or fund are used to purchase additional shares of that same stock or fund.

instead of reinvesting them he would have **less than half as much money**.

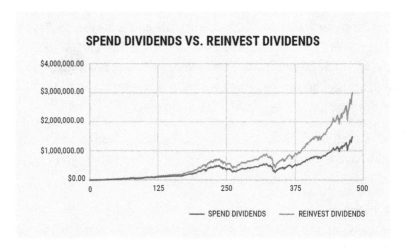

This shows just how important dividend reinvestment can be to stock market compounding.

Dividend yield is a financial ratio that estimates the cash return an investor can expect to earn from owning a stock or fund. Dividend yield is always expressed as a percentage. It is calculated by dividing a stock or fund's dividend payment per share by its current share price.

PART 7 REVIEW

- Compounding occurs when the proceeds from an investment are reinvested over and over again to generate additional returns. This causes the investment to get bigger at a faster and faster rate over time.

- Compounding occurs in the stock market because price movements are measured in percentages, not points.

- The percentage movement in the index is reset on January 1st each year. All of the gains or losses that are recorded in the following year use January 1st as a starting point.

- The S&P 500 returns are all over the map in any given year and are almost never exactly 10%. However, when viewed over long periods of time, the average annual return of the United States stock market is about 10%.

- Dividend reinvestment is when the dividends that are received from a stock or fund are used to purchase additional shares of that same stock or fund.

- Dividends play an important role in stock market compounding.

PART 8

GETTING STARTED

CHAPTER 33

DO I NEED TO SET UP A SPECIAL TYPE OF ACCOUNT TO INVEST?

I hope that you're now convinced that investing in the stock market is a great financial decision.

What's the very first step to get started?

The first thing you need to do is open an account with a brokerage firm. Brokerage firms are kind of like banks, except they enable investors to buy and sell stocks and other financial assets.

Opening a brokerage account is just as easy as starting a bank account. You simply fill out an online form, link your bank account, transfer some money, and you're up and running.

As to which broker you should choose, there are lots of great choices.

Here are five of the most popular brokers at the time of publication:

- Charles Schwab
- E*Trade
- Fidelity
- TD Ameritrade
- Vanguard

It's common for these brokers to offer promotions and bonuses for signing up, so be sure to shop around for the best deal. If you want more detailed information about which brokerage account is best for you, check out **brianferoldi.com/brokers** for an up-to-date list.

CHAPTER 34

WHAT TYPE OF ACCOUNT SHOULD I SET UP?

After you choose a brokerage firm, the next thing you have to do is figure out what type of account you want to open.

Broadly speaking, accounts fall into two different types: regular and retirement.

1. **Regular Brokerage Account**

    These accounts are funded with money from a checking or savings account. They receive no special tax treatment at all. If your investments make money through dividends or capital gains, you may have to pay taxes on your gains (depending on your income level).

    The good news about taxable accounts is that there aren't many rules to follow. Money can be moved in and out at any time. You can invest as much as you'd like. You can choose from a huge range of investment options, too.

    The only downside to taxable accounts is that they do not receive any special tax treatment.

2. Retirement Accounts

If you live in the United States and you're investing for retirement—as you should be!—there are more options available to you.

Retirement accounts offer investors extra tax benefits to help make it easier for them to save and invest for retirement. Some people refer to these as "tax advantaged" or "non taxable" accounts. The U.S. government provides these tax savings to incentivize people to save for their retirement.

There are many different types of retirement accounts available. Here is an overview of the four most common:

401(k): A 401(k) account is typically offered by employers for full-time employees. Workers usually sign up for these accounts when they first start the job, but they can enroll at any time.

401(k) plans offer several advantages that make them very popular with American workers:

401(k) pros:

- Contributions to 401(k)s are usually made through payroll deductions *before* taxes are paid. This lowers the employees' taxable income and provides an immediate tax savings.
- Many employers incentivize their workers to participate by offering a company match. This means that the employer will add extra money to the employee's account if they participate. This is, quite literally, free money for the employee.
- Money that is in a 401(k) grows tax-free.
- There is no income limit to participate.

- As of 2022, participants can contribute up to $20,500 per year to their 401(k). Employees over age 50 can contribute up to $27,000 per year.

401(k) cons:

- Taxes must be paid when the money is taken out of the account.

- The employee's investment choices are usually limited to a handful of funds that are chosen by the employer.

- The employee can't touch the money until they reach age 59½ without paying a penalty (except in certain circumstances).

Overall, 401(k)s are usually a great deal for employees.

EMPLOYER MATCHES ARE FREE MONEY

The majority of employers that offer a 401(k) or 403(b) to their employees also match a portion of their employees' contributions.

For example, a common matching program is "50% of employee contributions, up to 6% of total compensation." This means that if you earn $50,000 and contribute $3,000 to your 401(k), your employer will kick in an extra $1,500 on your behalf.

*That extra $1,500 is—quite literally—**free money**.*

If you are part of the 20% of workers who have access to an employer match and are not taking full advantage, please make that one of your top financial priorities.

Roth 401(k): These accounts are very similar to a regular 401(k), except the tax benefit is reversed.

Roth 401(k) pros:

- Many employers incentivize their workers to participate by offering a company match.

- Money that is in the account grows tax-free.

- There is no income limit to participate.

- As of 2022, participants can contribute up to $20,500 per year to their 401(k). Employees over age 50 can contribute up to $27,000 per year.

- There is no tax to be paid when money is withdrawn from the account.

Roth 401(k) cons:

- Contributions to Roth 401(k)s are usually made through payroll deductions *after* taxes are paid. That means that the employee does not realize an immediate tax benefit.

- The employee's investment choices are usually limited to a handful of funds that are chosen by the employer.

- The employee can't touch the money until they reach age 59½ without paying a penalty (except in certain circumstances).

Individual Retirement Arrangement (IRA): An IRA is nearly identical to a regular 401(k), except it is usually not associated with an employer. Anyone can set up an IRA with a broker and can contribute money to it on a pre-tax basis.

401(K) VESTING

Some employers build a "vesting" period into their 401(k) plans. A vesting period means that the employee gains ownership of the employer match after committing a certain amount of time to working for the employer (see Chapter 57).

Vesting periods are designed to incentivize employees to stay with the company for a long time.

For example, let's say a company has a 4-year vesting period on their contributions and that the employee gains ownership of the employer contribution at a rate of 25% per year.

Year 1: 25%

Year 2: 50%

Year 3: 75%

Year 4: 100%

If the employee was to leave after year 2, then they would only get to take 50% of the employer contribution with them.

Importantly, vesting does not impact the employee's contribution. It only impacts the employer's match.

Every vesting program has its own set of rules. Make sure you understand them before you sign up.

IRA Pros:

- Contributions to an IRA can be made through payroll deductions *before* taxes are paid. This lowers the employee's taxable income, which leads to an immediate tax savings. Contributions can also be made directly from an individual's bank account into the brokerage if it is not associated with an employer.
- Money that is in the account grows tax-free.
- There is no income limit to participate.
- As of 2022, participants can contribute up to $6,000 per year to their IRA. Employees over age 50 can contribute up to $7,000 per year.
- The account owner can invest in a huge range of financial assets.

IRA Cons:

- Taxes must be paid when the money is taken out of the account.
- The investor can't touch the money until they reach age 59½ without paying a penalty (except in certain circumstances).

Roth IRA: A Roth IRA is just like a regular IRA, only the tax benefit is reversed.

Roth IRA Pros:

- Money that is in the account grows tax-free.
- Money that is put into the account can be taken out tax-free at any time.
- As of 2022, participants can contribute up to $6,000 per year to their Roth IRA. Employees over age 50 can contribute up to $7,000 per year.
- The owner can invest in a huge range of financial assets.

- There is no tax to be paid when money is withdrawn from the account.

Roth IRA Cons:

- Contributions to Roth IRAs are usually made through payroll deductions *after* taxes are paid. Or, if not associated with an employer, the individual funds the account from their bank account. That means that they do not realize an immediate tax benefit.

- There are income limits, so some high-income earners cannot add funds to a Roth IRA. As of 2022, married couples who have an adjusted gross income over $214,000 ($144,000 if single) cannot contribute to a Roth IRA.

- The owner can't touch any of the investment gains until they reach age 59½ without paying a penalty.

Here's a table that provides an overview of the four main retirement account types.

	Contributions	Withdrawals	Income Limits
401(k)	Not Taxed	Taxed	No
Roth 401(k)	Taxed	Not Taxed	No
IRA	Not Taxed*	Taxed	No
Roth IRA	Taxed	Not Taxed	Yes

* Depending on your income

There are many other types of tax-advantaged accounts—403(b), 457 Plan, SARSEP Plan, SEP Plan, Simple IRA, Thrift Savings Plan, and more. Each of these account types all have slightly different tax benefits, rules, and regulations.

THE 401(K) WAS CREATED BY ACCIDENT

In 1978, Congress made a few changes to the U.S. tax code. One of those changes included a provision—specifically, Section 401(k)—that enabled employees to defer taxes on income that was invested in the stock market.

Ted Benna, a benefits consultant and attorney, discovered that the language was vague enough to be applied to thrift plans. He realized that employers could now combine the benefits of pre-tax profit-sharing plans with the employer matching contribution of thrift plans.

Benna convinced his own employer to offer this new benefit in 1981. Assets have been pouring into 401(k) plans ever since.

As of March 2021, Americans held more than $6.9 trillion in 401(k) plans.

CHAPTER 35

HOW MUCH MONEY DO I NEED TO HAVE BEFORE I INVEST?

A common mistake is to assume that you need a lot of money to start investing.

Decades ago, that used to be true. These days you can open up a brokerage account with $0.

Yup. $0.

Many brokers don't even charge their customers a commission to buy or sell, either. This means that customers can invest in the stock market *for free.*

What's more, some brokers allow their customers to buy fractional shares of stock. This means that you can buy ½ of a share, ¼ of a share, or even $1/10$ of a share.

The bottom line: you no longer need a lot of money to get started investing. Even if you only have $10, you can start investing.

WHAT SHOULD I INVEST IN?

There are several different ways that investors can put money into the stock market.

Investors can buy:

- Mutual Funds
- Exchange-Traded Funds
- Index Funds
- Individual Stocks
- Target-Date Retirement Funds

There are pros and cons to each.

Mutual Funds: Mutual funds are pools of money that are collected from a group of investors. Mutual funds are operated by a professional money manager whose job is to buy and sell a diversified group of stocks and other types of financial instruments on behalf of the fund's investors.

The good thing about mutual funds is that they are an easy way to invest in a large group of stocks at once. A few mutual funds do better than the market as a whole.

The bad thing about mutual funds is that the vast majority of them provide a lower return than the stock market over time. They are also more expensive to own than other types of investments, and they are usually tax inefficient, too.

Exchange-Traded Funds (ETF): An ETF is a collection of financial assets that can be bought or sold on an exchange, just like a stock.

There are thousands of ETFs for investors to choose from. Each ETF has its own investing approach that distinguishes itself from all of the other ETFs.

Some ETFs invest in specific industries such as energy stocks or technology stocks. Some ETFs invest in specific countries like Japan, Brazil, or China. Other ETFs invest in other types of financial instruments such as gold, real estate, or bonds.

The good thing about ETFs is that they are very easy to buy and can offer instant diversification. They can also provide investors with exposure to a specific type of investing strategy.

ETFs are usually less expensive to own than mutual funds. They also tend to be more tax efficient, meaning that the owner of the ETF will generally pay less in taxes than if they owned a mutual fund.

Index Funds: Index funds are very similar to mutual funds. They are pools of money that are collected from a group of investors that are then invested.

However, unlike mutual funds, index funds do not have a manager that is paid to hand pick the investments. Instead, index funds are designed to mimic the holdings of a financial market index such as the Dow Jones Industrial Average or the S&P 500.

Index funds also follow a buy and hold strategy. They don't trade in and out of the market.

The great thing about index funds is that they do better than the vast majority of mutual funds. They are also very low cost to own and very tax efficient.

Index funds have become an extremely popular choice with investors over the last few decades.

Individual Stocks: Some investors choose to buy and sell individual stocks.

The good thing about investing in individual stocks is that the investor has full control over what they invest in. If they buy good stocks, they can outperform the market over time. The investor also has control over timing of the buying and selling, so they have more control over their tax bill.

The bad thing about buying individual stocks is that it's up to the investor to do all of the research to figure out which stocks they want to buy. They also have to track the progress of their holdings to ensure that they still want to hold those stocks.

Target-Date Retirement Funds: Target-date retirement funds were created to meet the needs of an investor throughout their entire investing life. These types of funds were created to provide an extremely simple path for investors to save for retirement.

Target-date retirement funds are what is known as a "fund of funds." They hold a collection of other investing funds, each of which have their own investing risk profile objective.

Here's how they work: Each target-date fund has a specific retirement year associated with it. For example, the Vanguard Target Retirement 2045 Fund is designed for people who wish to retire around the year 2045.

Most funds invest primarily in the stock market when the retirement date is decades away. As the retirement date draws closer, the fund slowly shifts more of its assets into conservative investments. While this gradually lowers the fund's returns, it also helps to reduce the risk that the investor's portfolio will decline significantly right before the money is needed.

Their simplicity has made them a popular choice with investors, but like any investment, they have pros and cons that need to be considered.

The good thing about target-date retirement funds is that they are extremely simple and do a good job of balancing risk and reward over time.

The bad thing about target-date retirement funds is that their investing plans are pre-set and may end up being too conservative or too aggressive. There are also fees to be paid.

Overall, if you like simplicity, target-date retirement funds can be a great investment choice.

Here's a review of the different types of investment options and the pros and cons of each:

	The Good	The Bad
Mutual Funds	Instant diversification Chance to outperform the market Lots of choices	Most mutual funds underperform index funds Higher costs Tax inefficient
Exchange-Traded Funds (ETFs)	Easy to buy Instant diversification Lots of choices Low cost Some are tax-efficient	Some are expensive
Index Funds	Instant diversification Low cost Outperform most mutual funds Tax efficient	No chance to outperform the market
Individual Stocks	Lots of choices Chance to outperform the market Low cost	Very time intensive You might do much worse than the market
Target-Date Retirement Funds	Easy to buy Instant diversification One fund for life	Can be too conservative or too aggressive

DON'T MAKE THIS MULTI-MILLION-DOLLAR MISTAKE!

Some investors mistakenly believe that if they contribute money to a 401(k), IRA, or other type of brokerage account that they are automatically invested in the stock market. That's not always the case! In many cases, contributions are held in cash by default and are not invested in the stock market until the account owner chooses how they want the money to be invested.

Sadly, some investors have consistently put money into their retirement accounts for years only to later find out that the money was held in cash the entire time. Those investors ended up missing out on all of the gains that the stock market delivered during their career and they didn't even know it!

It's not a stretch to say this can be a multi-million-dollar mistake. Don't let this happen to you! Make sure you fully understand how your contributions are being invested.

CHAPTER 37

HOW MUCH DOES IT COST TO INVEST?

There are two primary ways that investors pay to invest.

Commissions: These are the fees that are paid to brokers for each transaction. Many brokers offer free trades these days, so there's no need to ever pay a commission.

Expense Ratio: If you invest in a fund such as a mutual fund, exchange-traded fund (ETF), index fund, or target-date retirement fund, you will probably be charged an annual fee to hold that fund. This fee is called an expense ratio, and it is based on a percentage of assets.

For example, a common mutual fund expense ratio is 1%. This means that if you invest $1,000 in that fund, it will cost you $10 annually to hold that fund ($1,000 x 1%).

A 1% expense ratio might not sound like much, but over time, it can actually amount to a lot of money.

Exchange-traded funds and index funds usually have much lower expense ratios than mutual funds.

Some index funds have no expense ratio, so you can literally invest for free!

The good news is the cost to invest has fallen dramatically over the last few decades.

WHY DO MOST MUTUAL FUNDS UNDERPERFORM THE MARKET?

Between 2004 and 2019, more than 89% of mutual funds underperformed the stock market as a whole, according to S&P Global.

In other words, the investors who owned those funds would have been better off if they bought index funds instead of mutual funds.

You might be scratching your head as to how this can be. Mutual funds are managed by professionals who study markets for a living. How can so many of them do worse than the stock market as a whole?

I'm convinced that this poor performance has more to do with the way that mutual funds are set up than the managers themselves.

Here are a few reasons why:

Misaligned Incentives: Most mutual funds earn money based on the total dollar amount of the assets that they manage, not based on the performance of the fund. A mutual fund with $1 billion in assets will make 100 times more revenue than a fund with $10 million to assets, regardless of how the fund performs. For this reason, mutual fund managers spend a lot of their time convincing investors to give them money instead of focusing on the best investment strategy.

Career Risk: To outperform the market, a mutual fund manager needs to be willing to invest in novel ways. However, when you invest differently than other investors, you run the risk of underperforming for long periods of time. If a manager performs poorly while investing unconventionally, they have a harder time justifying their actions. That increases their risk of being fired. This 'career risk' encourages mutual fund managers to invest conventionally, which makes it much harder to outperform the market.

Fees: Many mutual funds are actively managed, which means that a human makes all of the investment decisions. Mutual fund managers are well compensated, so the fund has to charge extra to pay their salary. The average mutual fund had an expense ratio of 0.66% in 2019, which is much higher than the 0.13% that was charged by the average index fund. That extra cost is a drag on the investor's return.

Forced Short-Term Focus: Many investors judge the performance of their funds over short periods of time (a year or less). If the mutual fund performs poorly during that time, then some investors will withdraw their money. When that happens, the mutual fund manager is forced to sell stocks at low prices, even if they don't want to.

The exact opposite occurs when a fund does well. Investors add money to the fund, which forces the manager to buy stocks at higher prices, even if they don't want to. These actions force fund managers to invest for the short-term even if they want to invest for the long-term.

Forced Diversification: Diversified mutual funds are not allowed to invest more than 5% of their fund in any single stock. If a mutual fund manager loves a business but it reaches 5% of the fund, they are forced to trim it and invest elsewhere, even if they don't want to.

Size: Mutual funds that are successful attract lots of money. As a fund grows, the manager has to make bigger investments. As a fund becomes larger it can influence market prices when it buys and sells. That can make it harder for the mutual fund manager to make good investments as it grows.

Taxes: Mutual fund managers do not pay taxes on successful investments; the mutual fund investors do. This incentivizes the mutual fund manager to ignore the tax consequences of their transactions.

When these factors are combined, it's understandable why most mutual funds underperform the market.

It's not because mutual fund managers aren't smart; the way that mutual funds are structured makes it hard for them to outperform index funds.

For that reason, index funds are the best choice for most investors.

SHOULD I BUY INDIVIDUAL STOCKS?

There's a lot of debate in the financial community as to whether investors should buy individual stocks.

The people who are for the idea point out that there are many reasons why buying individual stocks makes sense:

- The investor has full control over what they own, how much they own, what they don't own, and the timing of all their buying and selling.

- The investor can optimize their buying and selling to minimize taxes.

- If the investor picks good stocks, they can outperform the market.

- There are no costs to owning stocks.

These are all valid points. However, there are also plenty of reasons why an investor shouldn't own individual stocks:

- Finding, vetting, and buying stocks is a very time-consuming process.

- The investor needs to learn accounting, data gathering, data analysis, how to read financial statements, how to judge a management team, how to read SEC filings, and more.

- If most mutual fund managers can't outperform the market, what chance does an individual investor have?

If you are thinking about buying individual stocks, ask yourself these questions:

- Do you enjoy the process of researching individual companies?
- Are you an organized person?
- Are you willing to spend the time to develop a system that helps you identify good investments?
- Are you good at managing your emotions?
- Are you willing to lose money when you make mistakes?
- Are you willing to compare your results to the market to determine if your system is working?

If you answered "yes" to all of these questions, then individual stock investing might be for you.

However, if you answered "no" to any of these questions, then you shouldn't buy individual stocks. A better plan is to just buy an index fund or a target-date retirement fund.

It's worth mentioning that this isn't an all-or-nothing question. Lots of investors (myself included) split their investment dollars between index funds *and* individual stocks.

There is no right or wrong answer. The best strategy for you is the one that best matches your investment personality (see Chapter 50 for more information on this).

PART 8 REVIEW

- The first step to start investing is to open a brokerage account. Visit **brianferoldi.com/brokers** for an up-to-date list of brokers.

- There are two primary types of accounts: taxable accounts and retirement accounts.

- You can start investing with any amount of money.

- There are two costs to investing: commissions and expense ratios.

- The most common ways to invest in the stock market are mutual funds, exchange-traded funds (ETFs), index funds, individual stocks, and target-date retirement funds. Each of them has pros and cons.

- The vast majority of mutual funds underperform the stock market over time. This occurs because of misaligned incentives, career risk, fees, a short-term focus, size, and taxes.

- If the idea of researching and buying individual stocks interests you, go for it. If not, just stick with index funds and target-date retirement funds.

PART 9

ALL ABOUT FINANCIAL ADVISORS

CHAPTER 40

DO I NEED A FINANCIAL ADVISOR?

A financial advisor is a professional who can assist you with all areas of your finances. Good financial advisors can help with estate planning, financial planning, insurance, investing, retirement, and more.

It's never been easier to be your own financial advisor than it is today. The internet is filled with free online resources that can help anyone to get answers to any financial question that they can think of.

However, that doesn't mean that you shouldn't consider working with a **financial advisor**.

Here are some ways in which a financial advisor can add a lot of value:

- Help you deal with information overload
- Organize your financial life
- Provide a second opinion on an investment
- Prevent you from making an emotional financial decision
- Help you create an investment plan
- Connect you with other financial professionals that specialize in taxes, insurance, estate planning, and more
- Keep the big picture in mind
- Run different scenarios to help you make better decisions

- Give you peace of mind
- Help you determine if you're on track to accomplish your goals
- Help you make big life decisions
- Make retirement decisions related to Social Security, Medicare, and portfolio withdrawals

Of course, there can also be negatives to working with a financial advisor:

- They can be expensive depending on their fee structure
- Many financial advisors are not **fiduciaries**, which means they are not legally obligated to put their client's interests ahead of their own
- Many financial advisors are actually just salespeople

Whether or not you should hire one all boils down to this question: **Are you ready, willing, and able to spend time learning how to become your own financial advisor?**

If the answer is yes, you might not need to hire a financial advisor.

If the answer is no, hiring a financial advisor makes sense.

The good news is that this isn't an all-or-nothing decision. You can handle most of your financial life yourself and hire a financial advisor whenever you feel like you need help with something that is out of your comfort zone.

A fiduciary is a person or organization that is legally bound to put their client's best interests ahead of their own.

CHAPTER 41

HOW CAN I FIND A GOOD FINANCIAL ADVISOR?

If you choose to work with a financial advisor, it's **very important** to find a good one. There are lots of people that call themselves 'financial advisors' that aren't actually financial experts. They are really just salespeople who sell financial products.

Here are a few ways to find a credible list of financial advisors to interview:

- Ask your friends and family for referrals
- Ask accountants, tax professionals, and attorneys that you already know and trust for a referral
- Use websites like **Garettplanningnetwork.com**, **financialplanningassociation.org**, and **napfa.org** to find a list of potential advisors
- Many of the big brokerage firms (Vanguard, Fidelity, Charles Schwab) provide financial-planning services

Once you have a list of advisors, contact and interview at least three of them. Vet them by asking them all of the questions listed in the next chapter.

Hire whichever one you think is the best fit for you.

CHAPTER 42

WHAT QUESTIONS SHOULD I ASK MY FINANCIAL ADVISOR?

Hiring a financial advisor is a big deal. You are trusting this person with your financial life, so make sure that you interview them before you hire them.

Here is a list of questions to ask of any potential advisor:

1. Are you a fiduciary?

Being a "fiduciary" means that the financial advisor is legally required to put your needs ahead of their own. If they answer "no" to this question, do not hire them. Also, confirm that they are a fiduciary in all lines of their business.

2. Do you have any industry credentials?

There are dozens of certifications that can be earned through continuing education courses. It's a really good sign if someone is a Certified Financial Planner (CFP) or a Chartered Financial Analyst (CFA). If they mention other certifications, look up what those credentials mean on the internet to find out which areas of finance they specialize in.

Many certifications need to be maintained over time. Check the website of the governing body that issues the designation to make sure that it is still active. If it has lapsed or been suspended, find out why.

3. How do you get paid?

This is one of the most important questions you can ask. And yet, many financial advisors never discuss this with their clients!

There are a few ways that advisors can get paid:

- **Percentage of assets under management:** the advisor is paid a fee based on the total amount of assets that they manage for the client. The industry standard is anywhere between 0.50% and 1.25%. For example, a 1% of assets under management fee means that the advisor is paid $1,000 per year for every $100,000 that they manage. Some advisors charge lower fees as the assets that they manage for their clients grow.

- **Hourly fee:** a fee is charged each hour. It's common for a financial advisor to charge between $100 and $400 per hour.

- **Fixed fees:** a dollar amount is paid for each service performed. For example, they might charge $1,500 to $3,000 for a complete financial plan.

- **Commissions**: the advisor is paid a commission when a financial product is bought or sold. It's common to pay 3% to 6% of the asset's value.

- **Performance-based fees:** an additional fee is charged if a specific financial performance target is met. For example, they might charge an extra 0.10% to 0.75% if the portfolio does better than an industry benchmark.

Financial advisors often structure their practices in a few ways:

- **Fee-only:** This means that the advisor is only paid by their clients. They are not paid to sell any particular products. Under this arrangement, the client usually pays a fee based on a percentage of their investment assets that are managed by the advisor. They also might be paid an hourly fee or fixed fee for their services.

- **Fee-based:** This means that the advisor is paid by both the client and from earning commissions from selling certain financial products. This could include life insurance, annuities, mutual funds, or other types of investments.

- **Commission only:** Some advisors do not charge the client anything. Instead, they only earn a fee when they sell a product.

Ideally, you want to work with financial advisors that are fee-only.

COMPOUND INTEREST CUTS BOTH WAYS

Compound interest is an amazing ally when it's working for you. However, it can also be a bitter foe when it's working against you.

If you carry a balance on your credit cards, then compound interest is working against you. Credit card companies use compound interest to calculate your balance. Since the interest rate on credit card debt can be over 20%, your balance can grow quickly. If you're in that boat, getting your balance to $0 should be your top financial priority.

Another way that compound interest can work against you is through financial advisor fees. A 1% management fee doesn't sound like much, but it can add up hundreds of thousands of dollars over time. After all, if your portfolio balance grows to $1,000,000, then a 1% fee is $10,000 per year.

4. What services do you offer?

Will they help you with investing? Estate planning? Insurance? Be sure you understand what they can and cannot do before you hire them.

5. What's your investment philosophy?

Good financial advisors invest with a long-term time horizon. They buy assets and then hold onto them for years. They don't trade. They don't try to time the market.

If they tell you that their strategy is to trade rapidly, leave.

Ask them if they invest "actively" (in mutual funds) or "passively" (in index funds).

Ask them if they recommend buying individual financial assets like stocks and bonds or just sticking with funds.

6. How often will we communicate?

Everyone has their own communication style and needs. Some people want to talk to their financial advisor monthly. Other people only need to communicate once per year.

It's up to you to decide how often you need to communicate. Just be sure that both parties are on the same page.

7. How often will we need to meet in person?

It's common to meet more often in the beginning when you are still getting to know each other. After your account is up and running, meeting once per year is fine.

8. Do you have asset minimums?

Some financial advisors only work with clients that have a

minimum amount of assets to invest. For example, some might only take on new clients that have at least $50,000 to invest. Be sure that you understand this before you have your first meeting.

9. **How do you measure financial performance and investments?**

   Ask your financial advisor how they will measure your financial success. Ideally, it would be determined by whether or not you are on target to meet your financial goals. It might also be based on how satisfied you are as a client.

10. **Do you have a team that helps you manage my finances?**

    Some financial advisors will handle all of the work themselves. Others work with a team. Find out how they operate. If they work with a team, ask to meet with the other team members.

CHAPTER 43

HOW CAN I TELL IF MY CURRENT FINANCIAL ADVISOR IS ANY GOOD?

If you are already working with a financial advisor, it's important to figure out if you are working with a good financial advisor or just a salesperson.

Here are a few questions to ask yourself:

1. Have they ever discussed their fees with you?

The first question I ask anyone who is working with a financial advisor is "how does the advisor get paid?" More often than not, the client has no clue. The subject has never been discussed.

Can you think of any other service that you use where you have *no idea* how much you are being charged? If that sounds crazy, that's because it is!

If your advisor hasn't been forthcoming about the way that they make money working with you, find out right away. If they are hesitant to tell you, that's a sign that you are working with someone that you shouldn't trust.

2. **When they communicate with you, do you feel like they are educating you, or just confusing you?**

   Good financial advisors are teachers. They are knowledgeable about a wide range of financial topics and constantly work to educate their clients about how to best manage their money.

   Bad financial advisors are only trying to extract as many fees as possible. They often use industry jargon to confuse their clients.

   If you feel more confused after a meeting then before you went in, it's probably best to find another advisor.

3. **Are they a fiduciary?**

   If they are not a fiduciary, don't use them. Period.

   Why bother when there are many other financial advisors who adhere to the fiduciary standard?

4. **Do they communicate with you as often as you'd like them to?**

   If yes, great.

   If not, it might be worthwhile to find another advisor.

5. **How have your assets performed under their watch?**

   This one can be a bit tricky. It's common for clients to judge their financial advisor based solely on whether or not the account balance grows. That's *not* the way to judge their performance.

   Think about this: if the stock market is up 100% since you first became a client, but your stock market exposure is only up 50% over the same time frame, is that advisor doing a good job? No! You would have been much better off if you just put your money in an index fund.

On the other hand, if the entire stock market is down 20% since you started working with them, but your stock market exposure is only down 10%, they might be doing a great job.

You can't just look at your portfolio's performance in a vacuum—you need to compare it to an appropriate benchmark.

Finding a benchmark might be tricky. If you have a lot of your assets in cash and bonds, you can't compare your portfolio's performance to an all-stock index fund like the S&P 500. That's like comparing a horse to a Tesla.

Your advisor should easily be able to do this for you. They should also be able to explain in simple terms why your portfolio is returning at a different rate than the market.

If they can't, leave.

Unfortunately, leaving might not be easy. A lot of the worst financial advisors sell funds that do not transfer easily. They might also charge fees for leaving early, too.

Make sure you understand all of the costs before you pull the plug. You can try to negotiate with the advisor to see if there are ways to lower your costs.

If leaving isn't worthwhile but you are unhappy, stop giving them new money.

CHAPTER 44

WHAT ARE ROBO-ADVISORS?

The internet has enabled the creation of a brand-new type of financial advisor: **robo-advisors**.

Most robo-advisors keep things simple by investing in one or more index funds. The robo-advisors will often make small changes to the client's portfolio over time to ensure it doesn't sway too far from their goals and risk profile. Many robo-advisors can also optimize the portfolio to minimize taxes, too.

Robo-advisors offer a few big benefits over human advisors. The biggest benefit is that they are very inexpensive. Many robo-advisors charge an expense ratio of just 0.2% to 0.5% of the client's account balance annually. That's less than half of the typical rate charged by a human advisor.

A robo-advisor is a website or app that provides investors with automated financial advice based on a computer algorithm.

Robo-advisors usually have very low minimum investment amounts, which makes them accessible to almost anyone.

The downside to using a robo-advisor is that there's no one to talk to if you have specific questions. Some robo-advisors do allow their users to email or set up a call with people who operate the website, but there are usually fees associated with that extra service.

Here's a list of some of the most popular robo-advisors at the time of this printing:

- Acorns
- Betterment
- Bloom
- M1 Finance
- Personal Capital
- Wealthfront

Robo-advisors are catching on with investors, especially millennials. However, they are still new, so there isn't a long-term track to use as a reference.

If you're interested in working with one, be sure that you understand all of the details about how they operate before you invest.

PART 9 REVIEW

- A financial advisor is a professional who can assist you with many areas of your financial life.

- Whether or not you should hire a financial advisor boils down to this question: are you ready, willing, and able to spend time learning how to become your own financial advisor? If not, consider hiring one.

- Ask friends, family, accountants, tax professionals, and attorneys for a referral.

- Use websites like **Garettplanningnetwork.com**, **financialplanningassociation.org**, and **napfa.org** to find a financial advisor.

- Ask any financial advisor that you meet with if they are a fiduciary. If they say no, leave.

- Make sure you understand how a financial advisor gets paid before you become their client. Ideally, they are fee-only.

- Robo-advisors provide automated investment advice. They have several benefits that might make them a good choice, but they are still new.

PART 10

AVOIDING BIG MISTAKES

CHAPTER 45

SHOULD I STOP INVESTING IF THE ECONOMY IS DOING BAD?

Imagine that it is September 2008, which is when the U.S. financial crisis was really starting to kick into high gear.

News breaks that large banks such as Washington Mutual, Bear Stearns, and Lehman Brothers are failing. Foreclosures are skyrocketing. The stock market plunges. The unemployment rate begins to rise rapidly. Each day, the news only seems to get worse. Economies across the world are declining. Countries are having trouble paying their bills. Credit freezes up. Banks stop lending. Economic activity grinds to a halt. Everyone is scared of losing their job. 401(k) balances fall to multi-year lows. The situation gets so bad that the U.S. government is forced to pump hundreds of billions of dollars into the economy to keep it from collapsing.

Would you be interested in buying stocks?

For most people, the answer is no. They would be paralyzed with fear.

And yet, the best time to invest is when the economy is doing terribly.

That's worth repeating. **The best time to invest is when the economy is doing terribly.**

Don't believe me? The returns from the S&P 500 are *highest* when the unemployment rate is *above* 9%.

The returns from the S&P 500 are *lowest* when the unemployment rate is *under* 5%.

How could this be?

When the unemployment rate is high, the stock market has usually fallen drastically. This means that the P/E ratio has contracted and that stocks are cheap. When stocks are cheap, future returns are higher.

The exact opposite is true when the unemployment rate is low. Investors feel great, so the stock market rises. This means that the P/E ratio has expanded and that stocks are expensive. When stocks are expensive future returns are lower.

This is why it's a *terrible* idea to stop investing when the economy is doing badly. If anything, you should try to invest more.

CHAPTER 46

SHOULD I TRY TO TIME THE MARKET?

Between January 2000 and December 2020, that's two decades, the S&P 500 grew from 1,469 to 3,756, which is a return of 156%. However, the returns were anything but smooth.

The S&P 500 started January 2000 at 1,469. Then the fallout from the tech bubble of the late 1990s hit. By March of 2003, the S&P 500 was down to just 789.

The market recovered strongly between 2003 and 2007. By September 2007, the S&P 500 reached a high of 1,576.

That's when the housing bubble popped and the financial crisis hit. The stock market plunged. By March of 2009, the S&P 500 was down to 667.

The S&P 500 recovered strongly ever since. By December 2020, it was up to 3,756.

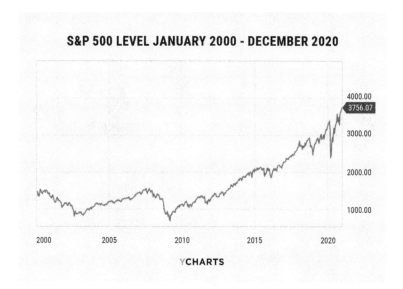

S&P 500 LEVEL JANUARY 2000 - DECEMBER 2020

YCHARTS

Wouldn't it be a great idea to sell before the stock market declined and then buy back in at the bottom? If you could do this, your returns would be huge!

Many investors try to predict the stock market's high and low points. This is called "timing the market."

I know how tempting this logic sounds. When you are looking backwards at stock prices, it's easy to identify the highs and the lows.

Unfortunately, it's *impossible* to figure out where the highs and lows are in real time. That's because there's no way to tell when the market is at its peak or at rock bottom.

That's because in the short-term, **market prices are controlled by the collective emotions of investors**.

Does that sound like something that you can predict?

Consider what happened in the S&P 500 between March, 1982

and December, 1996. The S&P 500 went from 113 to 741. The run wasn't perfectly smooth, but it was 14 years of the stock market going up.

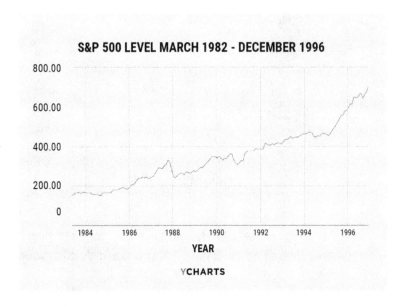

S&P 500 LEVEL MARCH 1982 - DECEMBER 1996

YCHARTS

Is the market at a top? It makes sense to think so. The stock market went up for 14 years in a row! Surely, it must be at the top.

Let's say you believed it was a market top and you decided to sell out of the stock market.

Was this a good idea? Well, one year later in December of 1997 the S&P 500 reached a new high of 962! If you sold in December of 1996, you missed out on a huge gain.

At this point it would be logical to assume that the stock market must be at a top now. The market has gone up for 15 years in a row! Sure, we sold out a little bit early before, but the crash must be right around the corner.

You can probably guess what's going to happen next. By December of 1998 the S&P 500 reached another new high of 1190! If you sold in December of 1996, you missed out on another year of huge gains!

You are likely thinking that we must be at a market top now. It's been 16 straight years of the stock market going up!

So what was the price of the S&P 500 one year later in December of 1999? 1,469! It was another all-time high.

Ask yourself: How would you be feeling if you exited the stock market completely in 1996? Keep in mind that you would have missed out on *several more years* of big market gains.

You would probably be kicking yourself. If you just left the money alone and didn't try to time the market, your returns would be higher.

But let's assume that you got lucky and nailed the timing perfectly. You sold everything at the exact top of the market.

That brings up another question: How do you know when it is safe to get back in?

Is it after the market drops 10%?

15%?

20%?

30%?

50%?

Let's say that you tell yourself that you will get back in after the market falls 30%.

What happens if the market only falls 28% and then completely recovers. What do you do now?

Do you wait for it to fall again?

This brings up the real problem with trying to time the market. **You have to be right twice**. You have to be able to sell before the big decline *and* buy back in before the market recovers.

Does that sound like something you can do in real time? Me neither!

When you are looking backwards at the history of the stock market, timing the market seems incredibly easy. When you are trying to do it in real-time, it's incredibly difficult.

The good news is that there's no need to time the market. If you invest on a regular schedule and hold for the long-term, the odds are extremely high that you will do great.

SHOULD I BUY PENNY STOCKS?

When I first started investing, I was drawn to penny stocks.

At the time, I only had a few hundred dollars to invest. I figured that it was better to buy a few hundred shares of stocks that traded below $1 than just one or two shares of a stock that traded for $50.

I used a simple stock screener to find stocks that traded below $5. I soon discovered that US Airways was trading for just $1.13 per share. Since I had flown on US Airways before and the share price was low, I figured this was a good investment.

Just a few days later US Airways stock price dropped to $0.75. I immediately became filled with fear, so I sold.

I'd love to tell you this was an isolated incident. It wasn't. I bought several different penny stocks and lost money quickly.

Was I just unlucky? I don't think so. I only later learned that the dollar price of a single share of stock is meaningless. It doesn't matter if you own 1 share or 1,000. What matters is how much capital you have invested in a company and whether the company is worth owning in the first place.

I also learned that good companies don't want their stock price to trade below $5. Low stock prices signal to investors that there is something wrong with the business. A low share price could mean that the company isn't profitable, is running low on cash, has poor business prospects, is being crushed by a competitor, or is facing a number of other problems.

As a general rule, if a stock is trading below $5, there's a good chance there's something wrong with the business.

You're better off avoiding it and looking elsewhere.

SHOULD I SELL A STOCK IMMEDIATELY AFTER IT GOES UP?

From 2004 to 2015, I worked for a company in the diabetes industry. That experience gave me a lot of first-hand knowledge about the various products that people with diabetes use to manage their blood glucose level.

In 2006, I learned about an up-and-coming technology called Continuous Glucose Monitoring, which makes it easier for people with diabetes to better manage their disease.

An early leader in this rapidly-growing industry was a small company called **Dexcom** (NASDAQ:DXCM). I believed that the company had huge potential, so in 2007 I purchased a few hundred shares of the company's stock at $6.67 per share.

My assessment turned out to be right. Continuous Glucose Monitoring technology became *very* popular within the diabetes community. Dexcom remained an industry leader and its share price soared. By the end of 2020, Dexcom's stock reached $403.67.

Unfortunately, I didn't participate in the huge gains. I sold all of my Dexcom stock in 2007 for $7.69 per share.

Why did I sell if I knew that the company had such huge potential? I was in a rush to take a profit. I saw the stock price going up and I wanted to cash in.

I'd love to tell you that I immediately learned from my huge mistake, but that wouldn't be truthful. I've sold lots of other great investments early because I was in a rush to realize a profit.

I've since learned that if an investment is going up and the opportunity ahead is still huge, don't be in a rush to sell. Selling a great investment early is one of the worst mistakes that an investor can make.

SHOULD I BUY THE STOCKS WITH THE HIGHEST DIVIDEND THAT I CAN FIND?

When I first learned about the dividend yield I became very excited. I did some quick research and found some stocks that offered dividend yields of 10%, 15%, and even 20%!

I said to myself "I should just buy the highest dividend yielding stocks that I can find. That way I'll earn a great return even if the stock price doesn't go up."

That's exactly what I did. And, like many of my initial instincts with investing, this strategy ended up losing me money.

What I didn't realize at the time was that **dividends are not guaranteed**. Since they are paid with cash, only strong companies can afford to make their dividend payments.

When a company has a very high dividend yield—say, over 5%—it is often because other investors are worried that the company can no longer afford to make its dividend payments. That worry caused the share price to decline, which in turn caused the dividend yield to rise.

Remember: the dividend yield is calculated by dividing a stock or fund's dividend payment per share by its current share price. If the share price is falling because the business is in trouble, the dividend yield gets bigger.

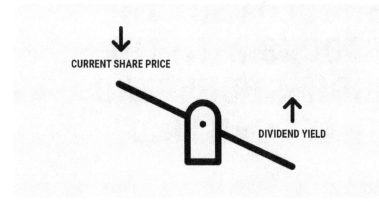

CURRENT SHARE PRICE

DIVIDEND YIELD

I didn't know this when I was a new investor. I thought that buying stocks with the highest yield was a safe strategy. In reality, it was very risky. The companies that I bought were in bad financial shape and many of them could not afford their dividend payments. As a result, many of them decided to stop paying their dividends after I purchased shares, which caused the share price to drop even more.

Talk about a double-whammy! Not only did I not receive the dividend payments, but the share price dropped, too!

If you're thinking "I should just buy the highest dividend yields that I can find," I urge you to think again. Remember: Dividends are not guaranteed.

PART 10 REVIEW

- If you invest in both good times and bad, you should earn good returns over time. Don't stop investing just because the economy is doing poorly. That can actually be the best time to invest.

- There's no magic signal that occurs at market tops or bottoms. Don't try to time the market.

- Remember, in the short-term, market prices are controlled by the collective emotions of investors. Does that sound like something that you can predict?

- If a stock is trading below $5, there's probably something wrong with the business. You're better off avoiding it and looking for a better investment.

- Don't be in a rush to sell an investment because it is going up. One of the worst mistakes that an investor can make is to sell a great investment early because they are in a rush to take a profit.

- Don't buy the highest dividend yielding stocks that you can find. A high dividend yield is usually a warning sign that the company can no longer afford to make its dividend payments. Dividends are not guaranteed.

COMMON QUESTIONS – ANSWERED

CHAPTER 50

WHAT DOES 'ASSET ALLOCATION' MEAN?

Pancakes are made from a few basic ingredients (eggs, milk, baking powder, flour, sugar, oil, salt). But you can't just put the ingredients into a bowl randomly and expect the pancakes to be good. Each ingredient needs to be portioned correctly. Otherwise, the pancakes will be terrible.

Your investment portfolio works in a similar way. A good portfolio is made of a mix of assets that need to be portioned correctly in order to provide the investor with what they are looking for.

There's a fancy term for figuring out what the right combination of investments is: **asset allocation**.

Asset allocation is an investment strategy that aims to balance risk and reward by optimizing the portfolio's mix of assets to best match the investor's needs.

Every investor has their own unique set of goals, risk tolerance, and time horizon. The goal of asset allocation is to optimize the portfolio's risk and reward dynamics to best match the investor's needs.

Broadly speaking, there are three main categories of financial assets that make up a portfolio:

- **Stocks** offer investors the highest long-term returns, but are also the most volatile asset.
- **Bonds** offer investors a lower return than stocks, but have much less volatility (more on this in Chapter 54).
- **Cash** offers investors very little return, but has no volatility.

If an investor is risk-averse and has a short time horizon, it's a good idea to keep most of the portfolio in cash and bonds. Their returns will be low, but the investor can usually count on the money being there when they need it.

If an investor wants a big return and has a long time horizon, it's a good idea to keep most of the portfolio's assets in stocks. The portfolio's volatility will be high, but the investor should earn good returns over the long haul.

It's every investor's job to find the asset allocation that best meets their needs.

In general, the younger the investor, the more aggressive they should be. The older the investor, the less aggressive they should be. However, every investor is different. Some investors have no problem handling market volatility. Other investors wouldn't be able to sleep at night if their portfolio's value dropped.

A good starting point is to subtract the investor's age from the number 110. The answer will provide an approximate target for how much of the investor's portfolio should be kept in stocks.

For example, if you are 30 years old, then you should aim to put 80% of your portfolio in stocks (110 - 30 = 80).

If you are 60 years old, then you should put 50% of your portfolio in stocks (110 - 60 = 50).

Of course, there are many factors that will affect this number. If you do not want volatility, invest more in bonds. If you want the highest returns possible, invest more in stocks.

A good financial advisor can help you figure out what your asset allocation should be.

WHAT DOES 'DIVERSIFICATION' MEAN?

There's an old saying "don't put all your eggs in one basket." The idea is that if something bad was to happen to the basket, you'd lose all of your eggs.

Investors can use this same logic to protect their portfolio from harm. An important way that investors can do just that is with **diversification**.

Diversification could mean that an investor holds a lot of different types of assets (stocks, bonds, commodities, real estate, precious metals). It could also mean that an investor owns companies from many different sectors of the economy (technology, communications, healthcare, industrials, energy, real estate, etc.)

Diversification means that an investor owns a wide variety of assets.

A well-diversified portfolio can help to smooth out the investor's returns. When some assets are performing poorly, other assets could be performing well. The two would offset each other and provide an overall return that was satisfactory.

When constructed properly, a diversified portfolio can actually lower an investor's risk and provide higher returns.

However, there are drawbacks to diversification. The more assets that are held, the more time-consuming it can be to manage them. Also, if an asset performs extremely well, but it's only a small part of the investor's portfolio, the investor won't benefit all that much.

Proper diversification is all about handling trade-offs. Investors should take diversification seriously.

WHAT IS 'REBALANCING'?

Imagine that an investor has a $100,000 portfolio. The investor decides to invest half the money in stocks and half in bonds.

Here's what the investor's portfolio looks like:

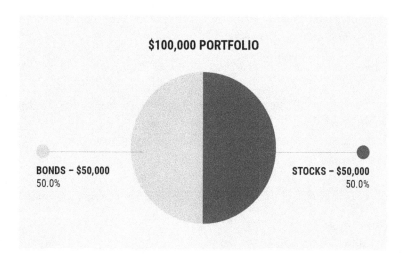

$100,000 PORTFOLIO

BONDS – $50,000
50.0%

STOCKS – $50,000
50.0%

A few years later, the portfolio's value has grown to $200,000. But instead of being at a 50/50 split, the portfolio now has 70% stocks and 30% bonds, and now looks like this:

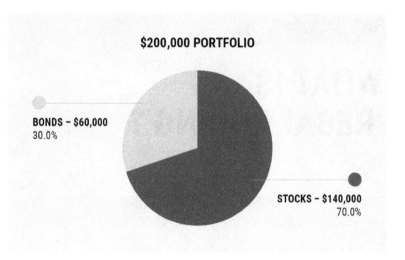

$200,000 PORTFOLIO

BONDS – $60,000
30.0%

STOCKS – $140,000
70.0%

The investor only intended to have half of their portfolio in stocks, but now has 70% of their portfolio in stocks.

When this happens, it is called an "unbalanced" portfolio. What that means is that the portfolio looks different than the investor initially intended. This happens because assets grow at different rates. In this case, the investor's stocks grew at a much faster rate than the bonds.

Rebalancing is the process of realigning the weightings of a portfolio of assets. Many investors like to rebalance their portfolio every year or so in order to keep their portfolio from becoming too dependent on a single financial asset.

To return the portfolio to its original state, it needs to be **rebalanced**.

In the example above, the investor would sell $40,000 worth of stocks and buy $40,000 worth of bonds with the proceeds. This would bring the portfolio back to its original weighting.

After rebalancing, the portfolio would look like this:

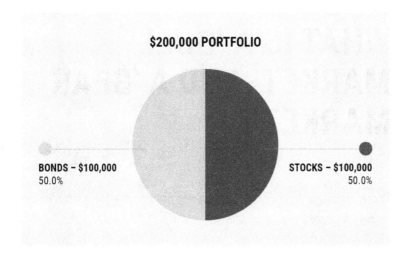

$200,000 PORTFOLIO

BONDS – $100,000
50.0%

STOCKS – $100,000
50.0%

While there are no rules about how often a portfolio should be rebalanced, many advisors suggest rebalancing your portfolio on a fixed schedule. For example, some investors like to rebalance their portfolio every year.

Rebalancing your portfolio can help to ensure that your asset allocation matches your risk tolerance level.

CHAPTER 53

WHAT IS A 'BULL MARKET' AND A 'BEAR MARKET'?

There are three directions that market prices can go: up, down, or sideways. Investors have created common names for describing all three of these market conditions, although there are four common terms associated with them.

When market prices are going up, investors call it a **bull market**.

A bull market is when market prices are rising.

The term bull market is generally used when market prices have risen by 20% or more from their recent low and are expected to continue going up. Bull markets tend to last for long periods of time. The term "bull market" gets its name from the way that a bull attacks; bulls thrust their horns in an *upward* motion.

Bull markets usually start after the end of a market period where prices are falling. While the length of a bull market can vary widely greatly, some bull markets have lasted for several decades.

When market prices are going down by a lot, investors call it a **bear market**.

Bear markets can occur for any length of time. There have been bear markets that are complete in a few weeks and there are bear markets that have lasted for decades. The term "bear market" refers to the way that a bear attacks its prey; by swiping its paws in a *downward* motion.

Another term that is commonly used to describe falling market prices is a **correction**.

> *A bear market is when market prices have fallen by 20% or more from their recent high.*

> *A correction is when prices fall 10% or more from a recent high.*

> *A sideways market is when market prices trade within a fairly stable range for a long period of time.*

Corrections in the stock market tend to be short-lived, lasting only a few months or so.

When prices are fairly stable, investors call that a **sideways market**.

Bull markets, bear markets, corrections, and sideways markets are most commonly associated with the stock market, but they also occur in other types of markets. There have been bull markets, bear markets, corrections, and sideways markets in bonds, interest rates, oil, precious metals, cryptocurrencies, real estate, and other types of assets.

CHAPTER 54

WHAT ARE BONDS?

You want to buy a house, but you don't have a few hundred thousand dollars in cash. What do you do?

For most people, the answer is to go to a bank and get a mortgage.

When companies or governments need money, they do the exact same thing. However, instead of calling it a mortgage, they call it a **bond**.

A bond is a debt that is issued by corporations, governments, or other organizations and is sold to investors.

Bonds are also called "fixed income" financial instruments. That's because the owner of the bond earns interest at a fixed rate.

There are lots of different types of bonds, but they break down into four main categories:

- **Agency Bonds** are issued by government-affiliated organizations
- **Corporate Bonds** are issued by companies
- **Government Bonds** are issued by governments
- **Municipal Bonds** are issued by states and municipalities

The exact details of each bond are unique, but they all have the following characteristics:

- **Coupon Rate:** the interest rate of the bond
- **Coupon Dates:** the dates when the interest payments are due
- **Face Value:** the amount of money that is owed to the bondholder
- **Issue Price:** the price at which the bond was initially sold
- **Maturity Date:** the date the bond has to be paid back

Bonds are generally viewed as lower-risk investments than stocks. That's because they have 'seniority' over stocks, which means they must be paid off first in the event of a bankruptcy.

While bond prices can fluctuate, bonds usually have much lower volatility than stocks. That makes them a good place to keep money for investors that do not want big price swings.

However, the tradeoff for that lower volatility is a lower rate of return.

CHAPTER 55

WHAT IS 'DOLLAR-COST AVERAGING'?

You may have heard the old saying, "Buy low, sell high."

In theory, it sounds easy and makes sense. In reality, it's just like trying to time the market. As we discussed in Chapter 45, timing the market is an incredibly difficult thing to do.

There's a simple buying strategy that allows investors to ignore market timing altogether: **dollar-cost averaging**.

Dollar-cost averaging is when an investor commits to buying a fixed dollar amount of a financial asset at regular intervals, regardless of the price at the time of purchase.

For example, an investor might decide to put money into an S&P 500 index fund every two weeks. The investor buys the fund no matter if the price of the index is up or down.

This strategy works wonderfully because there's no thinking. No second guessing. No wondering. The investor is always buying at the highs and the lows. Since the U.S. stock market goes up over time, the investor is likely to do very well by following this simple strategy.

Most 401(k) plans are set up to take advantage of dollar-cost averaging. Money is added to the market every pay period, which takes all of the guesswork out of when to invest.

Remember Aaron from Chapter 1? A big reason why he was able to turn $400 per month into more than $3 million dollars is because he took advantage of dollar-cost averaging. Aaron didn't even have to look at his brokerage statements. All he had to do was set up his account once and then forget about it.

That's the power of dollar-cost averaging.

CHAPTER 56

WHAT IS AN EMPLOYEE STOCK PURCHASE PLAN (ESPP)?

Natalie, Ethan, and Lauren decide that they want Best Coffee Company's employees to also become shareholders. They figure that allowing their employees to become shareholders will help to boost morale, make employees less likely to leave, and make them much more interested in making sure that the company is successful.

Employee stock purchase plans enable employees to buy their company's stock through regular payroll deductions, just like a 401(k). The employee's contributions are usually added up over a period of weeks or months and are then converted into stock on a regular schedule.

How can they incentivize employees to invest in Best Coffee Company's stock?

One way is by setting up an **Employee Stock Purchase Plan** (ESPP).

The exact details of the plan vary from company to company. In some cases, the employer allows the employee to buy the company's stock at a discount to its market price. The discount can be as much as 15%. Some ESPPs also have a "look-back" provision. This means that the employee can purchase shares based on the lowest market price during the offering period.

For example, let's say that a company's stock traded for $10 per share on January 1st. The stock appreciated to $15 per share by June 30th. If the ESPP discount was 15% and it had a look-back provision, then the employee would be able to purchase shares for $8.50 (15% less than the lowest share price).

If that sounds like it could be a good deal, that's because it can be. If you think your employer has a very bright future ahead, it can be a smart move to buy shares of the company's stock at a discount.

However, ESPP plans are not always slam dunks. If your company's stock performs poorly, so will your ESPP contributions.

There are also other factors to consider. You already depend on the company for your salary, benefits, and possibly a bonus. That means that your financial future is already tied to the fate of the company. It might not make sense to add more financial exposure to the company. (See Chapter 49 on diversification.)

Overall, ESPP plans can be a wonderful benefit for employees to take advantage of.

Of course, the exact details of the plan matter a great deal. Make sure you understand all of the pros and cons of participating before you sign up.

CHAPTER 57

WHAT IS 'VESTING'?

Many employers choose to add a "**vesting**" period to some of their employee compensation plans.

It is common for employers to add vesting periods to certain types of employee compensation such as a **pension**, 401(k) match, or stock-based compensation (more on this in Chapter 58).

> *Vesting is a legal term that means to gain ownership of a financial asset over a period of time.*

Vesting plans can be made over any period of time but the most common vesting periods for 401(k) matches and stock-based compensation are three to four years. The vesting period usually starts a year after the employee becomes eligible to receive this compensation. (Example: a new employee at a company may have to wait 90 days before they can sign up for the company 401(k) plan. Vesting would begin one year from that date, not the hire date, in some cases.) The vesting can be done equally over a set period of years, all at once, or in any other combination that the employer wants.

For example, let's say a company has a three-year vesting period on their 401(k) match. This means that the employee gains ownership of the employer's matching contribution at a rate of 33% per year.

At the end of the first year the employee would own 33% of the employer's 401(k) match. At the end of the second year the employee would own 66% of the 401(k) match. At the end of the third year the employee would own 100% of the 401(k) match. When an employee gains full ownership of the asset they are "fully vested."

A pension is a retirement plan in which the employer provides their retired employees with a monthly income. The employer takes on all of the risk and responsibility for funding the plan.

Vesting periods are designed to incentivize employees to stay with the employer for a long period of time. If the employee leaves before the vesting period is complete then they give up some or all of their compensation.

For example, if the employee in the example above chooses to leave in the middle of their second year then they would only get to keep 33% of their 401(k) match. If the employee left before their first-year anniversary date, then they wouldn't get to keep any of the 401(k) match.

Every vesting plan has its own set of rules. Make sure that you fully understand all of the details of any vesting plan that you sign up for.

CHAPTER 58

WHAT IS "STOCK-BASED COMPENSATION"?

Corporations compensate their employees in many different ways. The most common ways are with a salary, bonus, and benefits. However, some employers choose to pay their employees with **stock-based compensation**.

> *Stock-based compensation is when a corporation uses its own stock or stock options to reward and incentivize an employee.*

Stock-based compensation (which is also called "equity compensation") is very common in startups. That's because many startups cannot afford to pay their employees big salaries. They use stock-based compensation to make up the difference.

There are a few different types of stock-based compensation:

Performance Shares: a type of stock compensation that is typically paid to corporate managers or executives only if they met certain company targets. For example, an executive's performance shares might be tied to the company achieving a certain level of earnings per share or the stock price hitting some target.

Restricted Stock Units (RSU): a type of stock compensation that is issued by an employer to an employee in the form of company shares. The employee typically gains access to the RSUs after they work for the company for a set number of years. Once the employee receives their shares they can sell them at their discretion.

Stock Options: a type of stock compensation that gives the employee the right to buy shares of the company's stock at a set price in the future regardless of the stock's market value at that time. For example, an employee might be able to buy 100 shares of company stock for $5 per share over the next 10 years even if the market price of the stock goes up to $50, $100, or $1,000. Importantly, stock options give the employee the *option* to buy the stock if they want to, but the employee is under no obligation to do so.

It is common for stock-based compensation plans to be subject to a vesting period before it is earned by the employee.

Stock-based compensation can be very lucrative for employees if the company is successful. However, they can also be worth nothing if the company fails.

CHAPTER 59

WHAT IS THE FEDERAL RESERVE?

The United States has been dealing with economic booms and busts since it was founded.

In 1913, politicians decided that action needed to be taken to reduce the economy's volatility. The U.S. government passed the Federal Reserve Act, which created the Federal Reserve Bank (which is commonly called "the Fed").

The **Federal Reserve** was created to act as a regulator and supervisor of banks and the U.S. banking system. The Fed was given the power to issue and enforce regulations that control the lending activities of banks.

The Federal Reserve is the central bank of the United States. The Fed was created by the U.S. Government to provide the nation with a more stable monetary and financial system.

The Fed was tasked with two primary mandates:

- Maximize employment
- Keep prices stable

The primary tool that it has to manage both is the control over interest rates. Specifically, the federal funds rate. This is the interest rate that banks charge each other to borrow money.

The federal funds rate is the most important interest rate in the United States. All other interest rates are based on it.

Balancing its two mandates isn't easy. In general, when inflation is high, unemployment is low. When inflation is low, unemployment is high.

If the unemployment rate is high, the Fed can lower interest rates. This encourages businesses and consumers to borrow and spend. That drives economic growth and lowers the unemployment rate over time.

If the inflation rate is high, the Fed can raise interest rates. This makes it more expensive to borrow and spend. Economic growth slows down in response, which causes unemployment to grow and inflation to decrease.

The Federal Reserve must balance its two mandates in order to maximize employment without causing high inflation.

CHAPTER 60

WHAT IS THE SECURITIES AND EXCHANGE COMMISSION (SEC)?

The 1920s were a boom time for America. New technologies and industries were created, which allowed the economy to grow rapidly. The stock market soared to new highs in response to the prosperity.

The good times came to an abrupt end in 1929. The stock market started to fall. Economic activity began to slow. The unemployment rate started to rise.

What came next was an economic disaster. Banks started to fail. Construction came to a halt. Crop prices fell, pushing farmers into bankruptcy. Jobs disappeared by the millions.

Historians call this period the Great Depression. It was the longest, deepest, and most widespread economic downturn in the U.S. during the 20th century.

By 1934, regulators figured out that many financial institutions misled their investors prior to the 1929 stock market crash. At the time, financial markets were lightly regulated. That made it easy for fraud, insider trading, and other financial abuses to take place.

To ensure another Great Depression wouldn't happen, President Franklin Roosevelt signed the Securities Exchange Act of 1934 into law. The act created the **Securities and Exchange Commission** (SEC).

The SEC is kind of like the Food and Drug Administration (FDA), except it's focused on enforcing financial laws and maintaining healthy capital markets.

The SEC was created to help prevent future financial abuses. The agency helped to steadily restore Americans' confidence in financial markets.

The SEC still enforces financial laws today. Public companies are required to file reports and other information with the SEC on a regular basis. All of that information is freely available to the public.

The Securities and Exchange Commission is a federal agency that oversees America's financial markets.

CHAPTER 61

WHAT IS A 'STOCK SPLIT'?

Let's say that Best Coffee Company is successful. Its share price climbs all the way to $100.

Decades ago, this would have caused a problem. Brokers used to force their clients to buy and sell stocks in lots of 100 shares. If a company's share price went above $100, investors would have to buy and sell in $10,000 increments (100 shares x $100 per share).

That large amount of money was a barrier for lots of investors. To address this problem, companies would lower the price of their stock by performing a "**stock split**" whenever their share price got too high.

A stock split is when a company divides existing shares of its stock into multiple new shares of stock in order to lower the price.

A common stock split practice is for a company to divide each of their existing shares in half. When this happens, existing shareholders are given two shares of stock for each one that they own. However, the price of each new share is half of the old price. The net effect is that the total dollar amount that the investor owns is the same.

Stock splits confuse a lot of people. Here's an easy way to think about it: you buy a large cheese pizza that is cut into 4 equal slices. However, you wanted 8 slices. What do you do? You cut each slice in half. Voila! You now have 8 slices.

The total amount of pizza hasn't changed. The only difference is that there are 8 small slices of pizza instead of 4 large slices.

It works the same when companies split their stock. Let's say that a company is worth $16 and has 8 total shares of stock. This means that each share is worth $2.

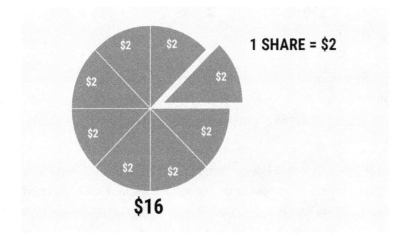

1 SHARE = $2

$16

The company then decides to do a 2-for-1 stock split. Each existing share of stock is split in half. Instead of having 8 shares of stock in total, there are now 16.

Since the entire company is still worth $16 and there are now 16 shares of stock, the price of one share fell to $1 per share.

Stock splits can be confusing, largely because the price of a stock is easy to look up, but the total value of the company isn't as easy to find.

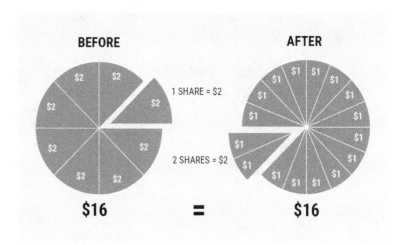

BEFORE

$2 $2
$2 $2
$2 $2
$2 $2

$16

1 SHARE = $2

2 SHARES = $2

AFTER

$1 $1 $1
$1 $1
$1 $1
$1 $1
$1 $1
$1 $1
$1 $1
$1 $1

$16

=

Let's go back to the Best Coffee Company example. The share price has grown to $100. Natalie, Ethan, and Lauren agreed that the share price was too high and decided to perform a 2-for-1 stock split.

Before the stock split, Natalie owned 6,000 that are worth $600,000; Ethan owned 3,000 shares that are worth $300,000; Lauren owned 1,000 shares that are worth $100,000; and public investors own 10,000 shares that are worth $1,000,000. There are 20,000 shares in total and the share price is $100.

Here's what Best Coffee Company's ownership looks like *before* the stock split:

Share Price: $100	Natalie	Ethan	Lauren	Public Investors	Total
Shares Owned	6,000	3,000	1,000	10,000	20,000
Ownership Value (Shares x Share Price)	$600,000	$300,000	$100,000	$1,000,000	$2,000,000
Ownership Percentage	30%	15%	5%	50%	100%

After the 2-for-1 stock split, the number of shares that everyone owns doubles from 20,000 to 40,000. To compensate for the doubling of shares, the share price is cut in half from $100 to $50.

Natalie now owns 12,000 shares of stock, but since the share price is now $50, the value of her stock is still $600,000. Ethan now owns 6,000 shares, but the value is still $300,000. Lauren now owns 2,000 shares, but the value is still $100,000. Public investors own 20,000 shares, but the value is still $1,000,000.

Here's what Best Coffee Company's ownership looks like *after* the stock split:

Share Price: $50	Natalie	Ethan	Lauren	Public Investors	Total
Shares Owned	12,000	6,000	2,000	20,000	40,000
Ownership Value (Shares x Share Price)	$600,000	$300,000	$100,000	$1,000,000	$2,000,000
Ownership Percentage	30%	15%	5%	50%	100%

The value of Natalie, Ethan, and Lauren's stock hasn't changed. Their ownership percentage hasn't changed either. Natalie, Ethan, and Lauren still own half of Best Coffee Company and public investors still own the other half.

The key point to remember is this: stock splits do not create any value for investors. They only increase the total number of shares and reduce the dollar price of a single share.

ADVICE TO MY YOUNGER SELF – AND TO YOU

ADVICE TO MY YOUNGER SELF – AND TO YOU

I hope this book has given you the information that you need to feel confident about investing in the stock market. This is the book **I wish I had** when I started investing, because I knew nothing at the time.

All of the knowledge that I have today about money, personal finance, and investing has been accumulated over years of reading, connecting with other smart investors, and my own trial-and-error.

I learned some money lessons the easy way. Others, I learned the hard way.

A question I often ask myself is: "what do I wish I could teach my younger self about money, personal finance, and investing?"

You'll find most of the investing answers in this book. Here are some other important money lessons that I wish I could teach my younger self—maybe they'll help you:

Saving is more important than investing

You can't invest without savings—period! If you're just starting out, focus most of your effort on growing your income and living frugally. Over time, your savings rate will grow, and you'll have much more money to invest.

Pay off your debts

Carrying debt doesn't seem like a big deal when things are going well, but debt can become a *huge* burden when life takes a turn for the worse. The future is unpredictable, and carrying debt adds financial stress to your life like nothing else. If you have debt, make it a priority to pay it off as soon as possible.

Track your income, expenses, and net worth

You can't make good money decisions without good information. This is why I'm a huge fan of tracking your income, expenses, and net worth. I don't care how you track these numbers—some people use software like Mint, Personal Capital, or YNAB; others do it all in Google Sheets or Microsoft Excel. Just pick a method that works for you and stick with it.

Compound interest can be a wonderful ally or bitter foe

Remember Aaron from Chapter 1? He turned $400 per month into over $3 million thanks to the power of compounding. If you can learn to make compound interest your ally, you'll eventually become wealthy. If you make compound interest your foe by piling up lots of debt, you'll never become wealthy.

Investing isn't just for the "rich"

Anyone can learn how to invest. It's not complicated, and you don't need a lot of money.

Don't let "analysis paralysis" keep you from getting started

It's common for new investors to constantly search for more information before they feel comfortable investing. The truth is that investing doesn't have to be complicated. Index funds plus dollar cost averaging plus patience is a winning formula. Don't let "analysis paralysis" keep you from getting started.

There is no such thing as a "perfect" time to invest

The news is always filled with negative headlines that might make you believe that right now isn't a good time to start investing. The truth is that there's never a "perfect" time to invest. Just get started.

Time in the market is more important than timing the market

The single biggest factor that will determine how well you do as an investor is how long you stay invested. Don't try to outsmart the market. Just invest on a regular schedule for a few decades and you'll be very happy that you did.

You don't need to pick your own stocks

I'm an investing fanatic. I love to research companies, value them, and buy them. I love the challenge of investing. For that reason, the bulk of my family's net worth is invested in individual stocks. However, few people share my affinity for the stock market. The idea of stock market research bores them to tears. That's perfectly fine! There's no need to buy individual stocks if you don't have the time or interest to learn how. Just buy index funds and call it a day.

Your biggest edge over Wall Street is patience—don't waste it

The only way to invest successfully is to invest for the long haul. Anything can (and will) happen to the stock market in the short-term. You must develop the patience to hold stocks when they are falling. If you let your emotions get the best of you and panic sell, you'll do poorly.

Penny stocks are priced that way for a reason, and it's usually not a good one

I was drawn to penny stocks when I first started investing. Thankfully, I had a really bad experience with them and lost what felt like a lot of money. That turned out to be the best tuition I've ever paid. I've since learned to avoid penny stocks. They are priced that way for a reason.

Invest, don't trade

It can be very tempting to buy and sell stocks rapidly to earn small gains. If you think you beat Wall Street at its own game, you should know that professional traders have faster computers and better information than you'll ever have.

Get started now!

There's an old Chinese proverb that says "The best time to plant a tree was 20 years ago. The second-best time is now." This is especially true of investing. A common regret I hear older investors make is, "I wish I had started sooner." I feel the same way and I was lucky enough to become interested in investing when I was 22. Get your wealth snowball rolling as soon as possible. You'll be glad you did.

GLOSSARY

401(k): an employer-sponsored account that provides workers with a tax-advantaged way to save for retirement.

A

Acquisition: when a company buys the majority of another company's stock in order to gain control of it.

Agency Bonds: bonds that are issued by government-affiliated organizations.

Appreciation: when the value of an asset increases over time.

Asset Allocation: an investment strategy that aims to balance risk and reward by optimizing the portfolio's mix of assets to best match the investor's needs.

B

Bear Market: when market prices have fallen by 20% or more from their recent high.

Bonds: debt securities issued by corporations, governments, or other organizations and sold to investors. Bonds are also called "fixed income" financial instruments because the owner of the bond earns interest at a fixed rate.

Bull Market: when market prices are rising.

C

Capital Gain: when an asset is sold for a higher price than it was purchased.

Capitalization-Weighted Index: is a stock market index in which each stock is weighted by its current market capitalization. This means that larger companies have more influence over the index than smaller companies.

Commissions: fees that are paid to brokers to perform a transaction.

Compounding: when the returns from an investment are reinvested to generate additional returns over and over again. This causes the investment to grow at a faster and faster rate over time.

Correction: when market prices fall 10% or more from their recent high..

Coupon Rate: the interest rate of the bond.

Coupon Dates: the dates when the interest payments on bonds are due.

Corporation: a legal entity that is separate and distinct from its owners. Corporations are owned by shareholders. The shareholders have a legal claim on the corporation's assets and profits, but are not personally liable for the company's debts or actions.

Corporate Bonds: bonds that are issued by companies.

D

Dilution: when a company creates new shares of stock, which has the effect of lowering the ownership percentage of the company's existing stockholders.

Diversification: a risk management investment strategy that mixes a variety of financial assets into a portfolio in order to minimize risk and maximize long-term returns.

Dividend: a payment of a portion of a company's profits to its shareholders.

Dividend Reinvestment: when the dividends that are received from a stock or a fund are used to purchase additional shares of that same stock or fund.

Dividend Stock: a company that pays a dividend to its shareholders.

Dividend Yield: a financial ratio that estimates the cash return an investor can expect to earn from owning a stock or fund. Dividend yield is always expressed as a percentage. It is calculated by dividing a stock or fund's dividend payment per share by its current share price.

Dollar-Cost Averaging: when an investor buys a fixed dollar amount of a financial asset at regular intervals, regardless of the price at the time of purchase.

Dow Jones Industrial Average: one of the first stock market indexes that was created to help investors figure out whether the stock market is going up or down. The Dow Jones is made up of 30 companies and is price-weighted.

E

Employee Stock Purchase Plan (ESPP): a company-run program in which employees can purchase the company's stock at a discounted price.

Exchange-Traded Funds (ETF): a collection of financial assets that can be bought or sold on an exchange, just like a stock.

Expense Ratio: a recurring fee that is charged to hold a fund.

F

Face Value: the amount of money that is owed to a bondholder.

Fiduciary: a person or organization that is legally bound to put their client's best interests ahead of their own.

Federal Reserve: the central bank of the United States. The Fed was created by the U.S. Government to provide the nation with a more stable monetary and financial system.

Financial Advisor: a professional who helps clients to manage their finances.

G

Government Bonds: bonds that are issued by governments.

I

Individual Retirement Arrangement (IRA): a tax-advantaged retirement account that allows individuals to contribute pre-tax dollars and grow tax-deferred. Taxes are not due until withdrawals are made during retirement.

Index Fund: a portfolio of stocks or bonds designed to match the composition and performance of a financial market index.

Inflation: when the price of goods and services rise over time.

Initial Public Offering (IPO): when a private company sells new shares of stock to public investors. The shares are then traded on a public stock exchange such as the New York Stock Exchange or the NASDAQ Stock Exchange.

Innovation: the introduction of new types of goods and services that open new market opportunities.

Issue Price: the price at which a bond is initially sold.

M

Market Capitalization: the current dollar value of a company's equity. It is found by multiplying the total number of a company's shares by the current market price of one share.

Maturity Date: the date the bond has to be paid back.

Mutual Fund: an investment vehicle that is made up of a pool of money collected from many investors. Mutual funds can invest in financial assets such as stocks, bonds, or cash and are operated by professional money managers.

Municipal Bonds: bonds that are issued by states and municipalities.

N

NASDAQ Composite Index: a stock market index that tracks the price movements of all the companies that are listed on the NASDAQ exchange.

NASDAQ Stock Exchange: an electronic stock market that was created in 1971. NASDAQ stands for the National Association of Securities Dealers Automated Quotation.

P

Pension: a retirement plan in which the employer provides their retired employees with a monthly income. The employer takes on all of the risk and responsibility for funding the plan.

Portfolio: a collection of financial assets that are owned by an investor.

Productivity: when humans find new ways to produce more goods and services with the same (or fewer) inputs.

R

Rebalancing: the process of realigning the weightings of a portfolio's mix of assets.

Restricted Stock Unit (RSU): a form of stock-based compensation that is given by an employer to their employee. Restricted stock units are usually subject to a vesting plan and are distributed after the employee achieves a performance milestone or stays at the employer for a certain length of time.

Robo-Advisor: a website or app that uses a computer algorithm to provide investors with automated financial advice.

Roth 401(k): an employer-sponsored account that combines the features of a traditional 401(k) and a Roth IRA.

Roth IRA: a tax-advantaged retirement account where taxes are paid on contributions and then all future withdrawals are tax-free.

S

Securities and Exchange Commission (SEC): a federal agency that oversees America's financial markets.

Sideways Market: When market prices trade within a fairly stable range for a long period of time.

Stock: a financial security that represents the ownership of a fraction of a corporation.

Stock-Based Compensation: when a corporation uses stock or stock options to reward and incentivize an employee instead of paying them cash.

Stock Buybacks: when companies repurchase shares of their stock from their investors. When this happens, the total number of shares that exist declines. This leaves all remaining shares with a slightly larger piece of the business.

Stock Market: a place where businesses and investors connect to buy, sell, and issue shares of publicly-held companies.

Stock Split: when a company divides its existing shares of its stock into multiple new shares of stock in order to lower the price.

Stock Market Index: a basket of stocks that are used to help investors track the performance of the stock market as a whole.

T

Target-Date Retirement Funds: a class of mutual funds (or Exchange Traded Funds) that regularly rebalance how much is invested in stocks, bonds, and cash to optimize risk and return for a predetermined time frame.

V

Vesting: a clause that an employer adds to certain types of employee compensation plans so that the worker gains ownership of the asset over a specific time period.

BIBLIOGRAPHY

Introduction

Jones, J. & Saad, L. (2021) "What Percentage of Americans Owns Stock?" *Gallup*. Online. https://news.gallup.com/poll/266807/percentage-americans-owns-stock.aspx Updated 8/13/2021. Visited 03/11/2021

Chapter 1: Why should I care about the stock market?

Elkins, K. (2017) "A brief history of the 401(k), which changed how Americans retire" *CNBC*. Online. https://www.cnbc.com/2017/01/04/a-brief-history-of-the-401k-which-changed-how-americans-retire.html. Updated 1/5/2017.

Terry, S. (1983) "Work experience, earnings, and family income in 1981" *Bureau of Labor Statistics*. Online. https://www.bls.gov/opub/mlr/1983/04/art2full.pdf. April 1983.https://dqydj.com/sp-500-periodic-reinvestment-calculator-dividends/

PK. "S&P 500 Periodic Reinvestment Calculator (With Dividends)" *DQYDJ*. Online. https://dqydj.com/sp-500-periodic-reinvestment-calculator-dividends/ http://moneychimp.com/features/market_cagr.htm

Jones, J. & Saad, L. (2021) "What Percentage of Americans Owns Stock?" *Gallup*. Online. https://news.gallup.com/poll/266807/percentage-americans-owns-stock.aspx Updated 8/13/2021. Visited 03/11/2021

"Compound Annual Growth Rate (Annualized Return)" *Money Chimp*. Online. http://moneychimp.com/features/market_cagr.htm

Chapter 4: What is the stock market?

"Wall Street Timeline." *History*. Online. https://www.history.com/topics/us-states/wall-street-timeline. 1/3/2019

Winck, B. (2020). "Here are the 10 biggest stock exchanges in the world, ranked by market cap" *Business Insider*. Online. https://markets.businessinsider.com/news/stocks/biggest-stock-exchanges-world-ranked-market-cap-nyse-nasdaq-trading-2020-6-1029325478#8-london-stock-exchange3. 6/19/2020

Chapter 5: What is the Dow Jones Industrial Average?

Hayes, A. & Perez, Y. (2021). "Dow Divisor" *Investopedia*. Online. https://www.investopedia.com/terms/d/dowdivisor.asp. 9/30/2021.

"Five Questions About The Dow That You Always Wanted To Ask" *Dow Jones Indexes*. Online. https://www.investireoggi.it/forums/attachments/five_questions_brochure-pdf.108747/

"Dow Jones Industrial Average." *Yahoo Finance*. Online. https://finance.yahoo.com/quote/%5EDJI/components

"Dow Jones - DJIA - 100 Year Historical Chart" *Macrotrends*. Online. macrotrends.net/1319/dow-jones-100-year-historical-chart

Financial Visualizations. *FinViz*. Online. https://www.finviz.com/screener.ashx?v=111&f=geo_usa

Chapter 6: What is the S&P 500?

Valetkevitch, C. (2013) "Key dates and milestones in the S&P 500's history" *Reuters*. Online. https://www.reuters.com/article/us-usa-stocks-sp-timeline-idUSBRE9450WL20130506. 5/6/2013.

"Our History" *S&P Global*. Online. https://www.spglobal.com/en/who-we-are/our-history

"Compound Annual Growth Rate (Annualized Return)" *Money Chimp*. Online. http://moneychimp.com/features/market_cagr.htm

Financial Visualizations. *FinViz*. Online. https://www.finviz.com/screener.ashx?v=111&f=idx_sp500&o=marketcap&r=21

Chapter 7: What is the NASDAQ?

"NASDAQ" *Capital.com*. Online. https://capital.com/nasdaq-definition

"NASDAQ Composite." *NASDAQ Global Indexes*. Online. https://indexes.nasdaqomx.com/Index/Overview/COMP

"NASDAQ Composite." *NASDAQ Global Indexes*. Online. https://indexes.nasdaqomx.com/docs/FS_COMP.pdf. 9/30/2021

Cunningham, S. (2020). "A Necessary Step:

All-Electronic Trading at the NYSE" *New York Stock Exchange (NYSE)*. Online. https://www.nyse.com/article/necessary-step-all-electronic-trading. 3/23/2020

Chapter 8: Why do companies go public?

Zachs. (2017) "7 Fun Facts about Starbucks In Honor of Its IPO's 25th Anniversary" *NASDAQ*. Online. https://www.nasdaq.com/articles/7-fun-facts-about-starbucks-honor-its-ipos-25th-anniversary-2017-06-26. 6/26/2017.

NVR. "NVR, Inc. Announces Fourth Quarter And Full Year Results." Online. https://nvri.gcs-web.com/news-releases/news-release-details/nvr-inc-announces-fourth-quarter-and-full-year-results-8. 1/28/2021https://nvri.gcs-web.com/news-releases/news-release-details/nvr-inc-announces-fourth-quarter-and-full-year-results-8

Sirius XM. "SiriusXM Reports Fourth Quarter and Full-Year 2019 Results." Online. https://investor.siriusxm.com/investor-overview/press-releases/press-release-details/2020/SiriusXM-Reports-Fourth-Quarter-and-Full-Year-2019-Results/default.aspx. 2/4/2020

Chapter 15: Why does a stock go up and down every day?

"McDonald's Fact Sheet." *M Investor Update*. Online. https://corporate.mcdonalds.com/content/dam/gwscorp/assets/investors/McD_IU_FactSheet_Nov_2020.pdf. 12/31/2019

Chapter 16: Why does the stock market go up and down every day?

"2020 Stock Market Crash." *Wikipedia*. Online. https://en.wikipedia.org/wiki/2020_stock_market_crash#13_March

"List of largest daily changes in the S&P 500 Index." *Wikipedia*. Online. https://en.wikipedia.org/wiki/List_of_largest_daily_changes_in_the_S%26P_500_Index

Chapter 19: How often does the stock market go up?

Housel, M. (2013) "Your Last Remaining Edge on Wall Street" *Motley Fool*. Online. https://www.fool.com/investing/general/2013/06/18/your-last-remaining-edge-on-wall-street.aspx. 6/18/2013

Chapter 21: Why has the stock market always recovered from crashes?

Resnick, B. (2011) "Recession as a Catalyst for Innovation". *The Atlantic*. Online. https://www.theatlantic.com/technology/archive/2011/10/recession-as-a-catalyst-for-innovation/246829/. 10/17/2011

Chapter 23: What is inflation?

De Maria, M. (2021) "What a McDonald's Big Mac Cost the Year You Were Born" *Eat This*. Online. https://www.eatthis.com/big-mac-cost/. 11/21/2020

"Why does the Federal Reserve aim for inflation of 2 percent over the longer run?" *The Federal Reserve.* Online. https://www.federalreserve.gov/faqs/economy_14400.htm

"United States Money Supply M0" *Trading Economics.* Online. https://tradingeconomics.com/united-states/money-supply-m0

"Top 10 Babe Ruth Cards of All-Time" *Cardboard Connection.* Online. https://www.cardboardconnection.com/top-10-babe-ruth-cards

Chapter 24: What is productivity?

Ball, E., Fugile, K., & MacDonald, J. (2007) "Productivity Growth in U.S. Agriculture" *United States Department of Agriculture Economic Research Service.* Online. https://www.ers.usda.gov/webdocs/publications/42924/11854_eb9_1_.pdf?v=3797.7. September 2007

"Nonfarm Business Sector: Labor Productivity (Output per Hour) for All Employed Persons" *Federal Reserve Economic Data - The Federal Reserve Bank of St. Louis.* Online https://fred.stlouisfed.org/series/OPHNFB

Chapter 25: What is innovation?

"Smartphones Market - Growth, Trends, COVID-19 Impact, and Forecasts (2021 - 2026)" *Mordor Intelligence.* Online. https://www.mordorintelligence.com/industry-reports/smartphones-market

Chapter 26: What is international expansion?

"Netflix Letter To Shareholders." Online. https://s22.q4cdn.com/959853165/files/doc_financials/2020/q4/FINAL-Q420-Shareholder-Letter.pdf. 1/19/2021

"Nike, Inc. Reports Fiscal 2021 Second Quarter Results" Online. https://s1.q4cdn.com/806093406/files/doc_financials/2021/q2/FY21-Q2-Combined-NIKE-Press-Release-Schedules-FINAL.pdf. 12/18/2020

"Dominos: Investor Data At A Glance." Online. https://dominos.gcs-web.com/static-files/60f2485f-43c9-42d2-b660-bc4ff0b4d654

"Apple, Inc. Form 10-K" *United States Securities and Exchange Commission.* Online. https://s2.q4cdn.com/470004039/files/doc_financials/2020/ar/_10-K-2020-(As-Filed).pdf

Chapter 27: What is population growth?

"World Population by Year." *Worldometer.* Online. https://www.worldometers.info/world-population/world-population-by-year/

"World population projected to reach 9.8 billion in 2050, and 11.2 billion in 2100" *United Nations*. Online. https://www.un.org/development/desa/en/news/population/world-population-prospects-2017.html. 6/21/2014

Chapter 28: What are acquisitions?

"M&A US - Mergers & Acquisitions." *IMAA*. Online. https://imaa-institute.org/m-and-a-us-united-states/

De la Merced, M. & Wingfield, N. (2017). "Amazon to buy WholeFoods for $13.4 Billion." *The New York Times*. Online. https://www.nytimes.com/2017/06/16/business/dealbook/amazon-whole-foods.html. 6/16/2017

Chapter 29: What are stock buybacks?

Abbott, J., Quintana, M., & Yardini, E. (2021) "Corporate Finance Briefing: S&P 500 Buybacks & Dividends"Yardini Research, Inc. Online. https://www.yardeni.com/pub/buybackdiv.pdf. 10/15/2021.

Chapter 30: What is compounding?

Schleckser, J. (2021)"Why Einstein Considered Compound Interest the Most Powerful Force in the Universe." *Inc*. Online. https://www.inc.com/jim-schleckser/why-einstein-considered-compound-interest-most-powerful-force-in-universe.html. 9/16/2021

Chapter 34: What type of account should I set up?

Cheng, M. & Segal, T. (2021) "What Are the Roth 401(k) Contribution Limits?" *Investopedia*. Online. https://www.investopedia.com/ask/answers/102714/what-are-roth-401k-contribution-limits.asp Updated 3/20/2021

"Amount of Roth IRA Contributions That You Can Make For 2021" *Internal Revenue Service*. Online. https://www.irs.gov/retirement-plans/amount-of-roth-ira-contributions-that-you-can-make-for-2021. Updated 6/21/2021

"Frequently Asked Questions About 401(k) Plan Research" *Investment Company Institute*. Online. https://www.ici.org/faqs/faq/401k/faqs_401k. 3/24/2021

Chapter 36: What should I invest in?

Hulbert, M. (2017). "This is how many fund managers actually beat index funds" *MarketWatch*. Online. https://www.marketwatch.com/story/why-way-fewer-actively-managed-funds-beat-the-sp-than-we-thought-2017-04-24. 5/13/2017

Chapter 38: Why do most mutual funds underperform the market?

Liu, B. (2019). "SPIVA US Year-End 2019 Score Card." *S&P Global*. Online. https://www.spglobal.com/spdji/en/documents/spiva/spiva-us-year-end-2019.pdf December 2019.

Chapter 44: What are robo-advisors?

Frankenfield, J. & Scott, G. (2021). "Robo-Advisor." *Investopedia*. Online. https://www.investopedia.com/terms/r/roboadvisor-roboadviser.asp Udpated 3/30/2021

"Pricing at Betterment." *Betterment*. Online. https://www.betterment.com/pricing/

Chapter 45: Should I stop investing if the economy is doing bad?

Yahoo Finance. S&P 500 Historical Data December 31, 1999 to December 31, 2020. https://finance.yahoo.com/quote/%5EGSPC/history?period1=946684800&period2=1609372800&interval=1mo&filter=history&frequency=1mo&includeAdjustedClose=true

Chapter 59: What is the Federal Reserve?

"Why does the Federal Reserve aim for inflation of 2 percent over the longer run?" *The Federal Reserve*. Online. https://www.federalreserve.gov/faqs/economy_14400.htm

Chapter 60: What is the Securities and Exchange Commission (SEC)?

"Roaring Twenties." *Wikipedia*. Online. https://en.wikipedia.org/wiki/Roaring_Twenties

"What We Do." *Securities and Exchange Commission*. Online. https://www.sec.gov/about/what-we-do#create. Updated 12/18/2020

Brock, T. & Chen, J. (2020). "Securities and Exchange Commission (SEC)". *Investopedia*. Online. https://www.investopedia.com/terms/s/sec.asp. 7/15/2020

RECOMMENDED RESOURCES

BROKERS

- Charles Schwab
- E*Trade
- Fidelity
- Interactive Brokers
- M1 Finance
- TD Ameritrade
- Vanguard

BOOKS

- *Choose FI: Your Blueprint to Financial Independence* by Chris Mamula, Brad Barrett, and Jonathan Mendonsa
- *One Up on Wall Street* by Peter Lynch and John Rothchild
- *The Dumb Things Smart People Do with Their Money* by Jill Schlesinger
- *The Index Card* by Helaine Olen and Harold Pollack
- *The Millionaire Next Door* by Thomas J. Stanley and William D. Danko
- *The Motley Fool's Rule Breakers Rule Makers* by David Gardner and Tom Gardner
- *The One-Page Financial Plan* by Carl Richards
- *The Psychology of Money* by Morgan Housel

- *The Richest Man in Babylon* by George S. Clason
- *The Simple Path to Wealth* by J. L. Collins
- *The Wealthy Barber* by David Chilton
- *Your Money or Your Life* by Vicki Robin and Joe Dominguez

INVESTING RESOURCES:

- cmlviz.com
- finviz.com
- fool.com
- morningstar.com
- stockrow.com
- finance.yahoo.com

To get a free copy of an up-to-date list of all recommended brokers, books, investing websites, podcasts, and more, visit **brianferoldi.com/resources**.

ACKNOWLEDGEMENTS

To my wife Katie, who has been my partner on this journey called life for 20 years.

Thanks to Tyler, Lindsey, and Madelyn, who always inspire me to live life to its fullest.

Thanks to Ken Feroldi and Nancy Feroldi, who have always believed in me.

Thanks to David Gardner and Tom Gardner, who created an amazing company that has greatly enriched my life.

Thanks to Anand Chokkavelu, Robyn Gearey, Michael Douglass, and Kristine Harjes, who were willing to take a chance on a new writer with poor spelling and grammar skills.

Thanks to Morgan Housel and Brian Stoffel, who inspired me to write this book.

Thanks to MK Williams, Brad Barrett, and Jonathan Mendonsa, who were willing to take a chance on a new author.

Thanks to Karsten Jeske (aka Big ERN) for helping me make sense of all of the historic stock market data.

Thanks to Lisa Messina, Jamie Orsi, Mike and Kim Calise, Courtney Morrosetti, Steve Raymond, Heather Snow, Ed Vallante, and all of my friends, family, and followers who gave up their precious free time to help make this book better.

ABOUT THE AUTHOR

Brian Feroldi is a financial educator, podcaster, YouTuber, speaker, writer, and now author—which is ironic because he is terrible at spelling and grammar. Weep for his editors.

Brian's mission is "to spread financial wellness." He does so by writing articles for The Motley Fool, appearing on podcasts and live streams, and sharing his thoughts on social media. He loves to connect with other investors online, especially on Fool.com, YouTube, and Twitter.

Brian has called Rhode Island home for most of his life and has been happily married for more than 15 years. He has three children who bring him tremendous joy and keep him on his toes.

Brian's favorite things to do are hang out with friends and family, watch his kids play sports, play games, listen to podcasts, dominate at trivia, have meaningful conversations around campfires, and volunteer in his community.

ATTENTION: Quantity discounts are available to your company, educational institution, or writing organization for reselling, educational purposes, subscription incentives, gifts, or fundraiser campaigns.

Brian Feroldi is also available for speaking. If you are interested in hiring him, please contact him at the information provided below.

Email: brian@brianferoldi.com
Twitter: @brianferoldi
YouTube: /brianferoldiyt
LinkedIn: /in/brianferoldi/
Instagram: @brianferoldi
Web: brianferoldi.com

ANOTHER GREAT READ FROM CHOOSE FI PUBLISHING

Read the book from the award-winning podcast ChooseFI, credited with sparking the Financial Independence Movement that is sweeping the globe.

If you are in debt, bad with money, or looking for a straightforward way to take command of your finances, this book is for you. This isn't just another personal finance book or budgeting guide telling you how to live like someone else. This book will give you the framework for success from dozens of people who have found their own path to financial independence.

Choose FI: Your Blueprint to Financial Independence makes managing your money simple, accessible, and actionable.

Anyone can follow these simple, common-sense lessons - the key is to take action! Get started on your path to Financial Independence today.

choosefi.com/book